What Sponsors Say About Supporting Native Missionaries

"I believe that missions is one of the hardest things
for Western Christians to relate to,
because from our childhood we are raised to be
materialistic and self-centered.
This is not God's purpose!
Our church's involvement with Gospel for Asia
has done two dramatic things:
First, our life-style has changed.
We are now missions-conscious on a
worldwide scale. Our people are getting
beyond their own backyards.
Second, we are more carefully examining
each dollar we send for missions and asking,
'Is there waste involved here?'
We support sixty native missionaries
through Gospel for Asia,
and the families here are having a chance
to be connected with believers in the Third World.
They see their pictures,
read their testimonies
and pray for them.
I am so very appreciative of
our involvement with Gospel for Asia."
—*Pastor L. B.*
Yuba City, California

"I was saved when I was thirty years old.
My salvation experience was dramatic,
and my life was turned completely around.
I really feel that I know what it's like to be lost,
and I have a tremendous burden for the unreached —
those who have never heard about Jesus.
When I found out about Gospel for Asia,
I was so excited to know
that I could play a significant part.
I know that through my support thousands
can come to know Jesus instead of slipping into hell.
I rejoice to know that I am storming
the gates of hell and impacting eternity."
—*Miss J. F.*
Chicago, Illinois

"Our family has been quite involved in supporting
native missionaries through Gospel for Asia
(in fact, our kids each support one).
We live in a small Midwestern town,
and we've never really traveled much;
so when the Lord brought this opportunity
across our path, our perspectives really changed!
We became less self-centered,
our burden for the lost
in unreached lands greatly increased,
and we grew much more eternally minded.
Now we are hungry to know more
of the Lord's will for our lives.
Our constant prayer is,
'Lord, use us. What more can we do for You?' "
—*Mr. and Mrs. T. G. and family*
Holdrege, Nebraska

The Impact of
This Book

Here's just a sampling of responses we've received over the past eight years from Christians who have read *Revolution in World Missions*:

"I have just read *Revolution in World Missions*.
This book greatly ministered to me
and stirred me in a way no book has ever done.
How can we order more copies?"
—*Pastor J. P.*
Lakeside, Oregon

"I was a missionary in Nigeria for twenty years
and understand what this book is all about."
—*Mrs. D. T.*
Kearney, Arizona

"Your book stirred me to tears
and drove me to prayer!
Please send me more information
about your ministry to native missionaries.
May God continue to bless you and use you."
—*Miss J. S.*
Towson, Maryland

"I have just finished reading your book,
and I have been deeply stirred by it.
I am eligible for Social Security this year,
and my husband is going to let me use
all of my monthly check for missions.
We will live on his Social Security and pension.
It is amazing how the Lord stretches our funds.
But our life-style is simple,
and giving is our greatest joy."
—*Mrs. D. F.*
Binghamton, New York

"I read your book and think it is one of the
most dynamic, down-to-earth books
that I have ever read.
I want to give a copy to our pastor,
each board member and
selected other people at our church."
—*Mr. P.W.*
Santa Margarita, California

"I just finished reading *Revolution in
World Missions* by K.P. Yohannan.
The thought that for the cost of supporting
one missionary from Canada
as many as ten local Asian missionaries
could be supported continues to astound me."
—*Mr. S. D.*
Calgary, Alberta

"We both read K.P.'s book
and were very moved
to change part of our life-style
to further the gospel.
I hope we can do more as we get braver!"
—*Mr. and Mrs. D. F.*
Los Alamos, New Mexico

"I saw myself too many times
in your book, K.P.
Although we are going through
a financial trial right now,
I realize how very blessed we are
compared to most of the rest of the world.
I have caught sight of your vision."
—*Mrs. S. S.*
Chesapeake, Virginia

"After finishing your book,
our family is now deciding how
we can be a part of God's plan
for His church in Asia.
If you have any suggestions,
we would enjoy your input —
especially from the experience
you have acquired."
—*Mr. P. P.*
Fort Atkinson, Wisconsin

"We have been challenged and convicted
by *Revolution in World Missions*.
We believe that our Lord Jesus is offering us
the chance to share in His work in Asia —
a chance we don't want to miss!"
—*Mr. and Mrs. M. D.*
Pacifica, California

"After reading *Revolution in World Missions*
I am convinced our small amount
of money can do more good
in this mission than
many others we participate in."
—*Mrs. I. T.*
Houston, Texas

Revolution in World Missions

To open their eyes, and
to turn them from darkness to light,
and from the power of Satan to God,
that they may receive forgiveness
of sins, and inheritance among
them that are sanctified by faith.

— Acts 26:18

Revolution in World Missions

K. P. YOHANNAN

CREATION HOUSE

Strang Communications Company
Altamonte Springs, Florida

Creation House
Strang Communications Company
190 North Westmonte Drive
Altamonte Springs, FL 32714
(407) 862-7565

Unless otherwise noted, all Scripture quotations are from the
King James Version of the Bible.

Scripture quotations marked NIV are from the Holy Bible,
New International Version. Copyright © 1973, 1978, 1984,
International Bible Society. Used by permission.

First printing, July 1986
Second printing, November 1986
Third printing, May 1987
Fourth printing, December 1987
Revised edition, July 1989
First printing pocketsize, May 1991
Second printing pocketsize, January 1992
Third printing pocketsize, June 1992

*This book is dedicated to George Verwer, founder
and international director of Operation Mobilization,
whom the Lord used to call me into the ministry
and whose life and example have influenced me
more than any other single individual's.*

Acknowledgments

There are hundreds of people who have had an impact on this volume — from those who have made suggestions, to those who have given encouragement, to those who have influenced my life and ministry. To all of them — all of you — I want to thank you and thank the Lord for placing you in my path.

Of those especially close to me during the long writing, editing and review of this manuscript, I would like to thank William T. Bray, David and Karen Mains, Gayle Erwin, Dave Hicks and Martin Bennett for their honest criticism and unwavering support of this entire project.

Special thanks also are due Margaret Jordan, Heidi Chupp and Jenifer George, who typed the manuscript, and to Larry Jerden for his contributions to the introduction and for his overall management of its production.

Most of all, of course, my greatest debt is to my wife, Gisela, for her careful reading of all that was written and for her suggestions that made the critical difference in several passages. Most of all, her emotional and spiritual support made the writing of this book possible. Without her standing beside me and encouraging me during these eventful years, this book — and the message it proclaims — would not have been possible.

K.P. Yohannan

Contents

Part III: The Way

Foreword

by David and Karen Mains

We all are skeptical of Christians with big dreams. We don't know why exactly — perhaps we have met too many who pursued visions but whose personal lives were nightmares.

The first time we remember meeting K.P. Yohannan we brought him home for dinner, and our family dragged this slight Indian along with us to a high school gymnasium to sit through an American rite of passage — an all-school spaghetti supper. Across the paper tablecloth, the garlic bread and the center-pieces — shellacked lunch sacks filled with an assortment of dried weeds and pasta (created by members of the Mains family!) — we heard of a dream to win not only India but all of Asia for Christ.

Since that evening in the noisy gymnasium in West Chicago, Illinois, there have been many more shared experiences — phone calls from Dallas; trips to the cities and backwaters of India; pastors' conferences in open thatched-roofed, bamboo-sided pavilions; laughter; travel on Third World roads; and times of prayer.

Very simply said, we have come to believe in K.P.

And we believe in his plan for evangelization which, with the profundity of simplicity, bypasses the complexity of technology and challenges Asians to give up their lives to win their fellow countrymen to Christ.

This book, *Revolution in World Missions*, reveals one of God's

17

master plans to reach the world before the end of time. With absolute confidence we know we can endorse the integrity of its author, a man of God, and we are thrilled with the work of Gospel for Asia.

You can read knowing that those evangelists traveling into the unreached villages of Asia have more heart, more fervor, more passion to spread the gospel of Christ than most of us who are surrounded by the comforts and conveniences of our Western world.

We know because we have seen them and talked with them, and they have put us to shame.

It is the internationals who are the wave of the missionary effort of the future. K.P. Yohannan's book paints the picture of how that dream can become reality.

This is one dreamer of whom we are no longer skeptical. We think you will find reason to believe as well.

Introduction

Revised Edition, 1992

Before the second half of the 1980s rolled around, most evangelical Christians in Western countries tended to view mission history in terms of only two great waves of activity.

The first wave broke over the New Testament world in the first century as the apostles obeyed the Great Commission. It swept through the Jewish and pagan communities of the Roman Empire, bringing the message of salvation to all of the Mediterranean world, much of Southern Europe and even some parts of Asia.

The second wave was most often dated from William Carey's pioneer work in eighteenth-century India. It began a flood of nineteenth- and twentieth-century missions to the colonies of the great European powers. Although World War II marked the end of this colonial era, it still frequently defines the image of missions for many Western Christians.

But around the world today, this definition is fast disappearing as the Holy Spirit is breaking over Asian and African nations, raising up a new army of missionaries. These humble, obscure pioneers of the gospel are taking up the banner of the cross where colonial-era missions left off.

This third wave is the native missionary movement. Thousands of dedicated men and women are bringing the salvation story to their own people — millions of lost souls in closed countries who would probably never learn about the love of God by any other means.

As Christians in the West gradually develop a greater understanding of what this third wave means to world evangelism, it becomes a potent challenge to our attitudes and life-styles. Thousands of individuals and churches are becoming senders of native missionaries, praying and supporting them on the frontiers of faith.

Revolution in World Missions has undergone various revisions over the past eight years. I have sought to clarify basic areas of misunderstanding surrounding the native missionary movement, such as the changing role of Western missionaries and standards of accountability in native missions. By printing a pocket-sized edition at a much lower cost, we have also made it more available to the public.

The impact this book has made continues to grow. Pastors have written us, testifying of the dramatic changes their church's mission programs have had. Fathers and mothers — and their children — are learning to live more simply and creatively in order to support native missionaries. Young adults, faced with eternal matters, are choosing to make their lives count for the kingdom rather than succumb to the climb up the ladder.

I believe we will see this generation reached for Christ as this exciting third wave of mission leadership unites with concerned Christians and churches around the world. As we draw nearer to Christ in unity, feeling His heartbeat for lost and dying souls, we realize that we are all serving one King and one kingdom. May this book serve to bring greater unity and cooperation among all God's people, as we seek to obey His will together.

K.P. Yohannan

Part I

THE VISION

1

How Many Would Be Beaten
and Go Hungry?

The silence of the great hall in Cochin was broken only by soft choking sobs. The Spirit of God was moving over the room with awesome power — convicting of sin and calling men and women into His service. Before the meeting ended, 120 of the 1,200 pastors and Christian leaders present made their way to the altar, responding to the "call of the North."

They were not saying, "I'm willing to go," but "I am going."

They made the choice to leave home, village and family, business or career and go where they would be hated and feared. Meanwhile, another six hundred pastors pledged to return to their congregations and raise up more missionaries who would leave South India and go to the North.

I stood silently in the holy hush, praying for the army of God crowded around the altar. I was humbled by the presence of God.

As I prayed, my heart ached for these men who came to the altar. How many would be beaten and go hungry or be cold and lonely in the years ahead? How many would sit in jails for their faith? I prayed for the blessing and protection of God on them — and for more sponsors across the seas to stand with them.

They were leaving many material comforts, family ties and personal ambitions. Ahead lay a new life among strangers. But also I knew there would be spiritual victory as they would witness many thousands turn to Christ and help to form new congregations in the unreached villages of North India.

How different were my tears now from those on that fateful day of decision back in 1973. Then I sat on a Punjabi curbstone blinded by the bitter tears of frustration and failure. Today tears of joy trickled down my cheeks as I realized how God had turned my despair into victory. Out of that crisis of discouragement, the God of Abraham had answered prayers. Here before my eyes was proof He is creating a third wave in missions — calling native believers to the harvest field.

With me in the meeting was U.S. Christian radio broadcaster David Mains, a serious student of revival. He had joined us in Cochin as one of the conference speakers. He later testified how the Lord had taken over the meeting in a most unusual way.

"It would hardly have been different," he wrote later, "had Jesus Himself been bodily among us. The spirit of worship filled the hall. The singing was electrifying. The power of the Holy Spirit came upon the audience. Men actually groaned aloud. I have read of such conviction in early American history during the times like the two Great Awakenings, but I had never anticipated experiencing it firsthand."

But the Lord isn't simply calling out a huge army of native workers. God is at work saving people from sin in numbers we never before dreamed possible. People are coming to Christ all across Asia at an accelerated rate wherever salvation is being proclaimed. In some areas — like India, Indonesia, the Philippines and Thailand — it is not uncommon now for the Christian community to grow as much in only one month as it formerly did in a whole year.

If anything, I have found reports of mass conversion and church growth are being underplayed in the Western press. The exciting truth about God's working in Asia has yet to be told. This dearth of information about what is happening in most countries is partly because the press has limited access. Except for in a few countries, like Korea and the Philippines, the real story is not getting out.

A remarkable movement to Christ is developing in the North

Indian state of Rajasthan, known as the "land of kings." We started work in this area with a team of South Indian native evangelists in 1965. At that time it was known in our language as the "wilderness of the gospel." For hundreds of years, British and American missionaries had carried on educational and medical work in this area. However, there was never any true indigenous church movement. But now, in just three months, we have seen new churches planted in twenty-one villages. In a major provincial capital, over one thousand came to Christ in one week alone! In my opinion, this is a miraculous movement of the Holy Spirit similar to accounts in the book of Acts or in early church history.

When you think of the past record, the progress is staggering. The people of this state have resisted the gospel for centuries. Many Christians have been seriously injured in riots caused by angry mobs who oppose the preaching of Christ. Some have even died for their faith.

These new church growth movements are being led by unknown bands of native evangelists who have never had one line of publicity in the Western press.

Typical of the many native missionary movements that have sprung up overnight is the work in the Punjab of a native brother from Kerala. A former military officer who gave up a commission and army career to help start a gospel team, he now leads more than four hundred full-time missionaries. Recently I received a request from him asking us to sponsor another one hundred helpers. Ten years ago we would have been happy to see three or four workers raised up. But now, thanks to the support that has been coming through Gospel for Asia, he has been able to accept a steady stream of new staff from South India.

Like other native mission leaders, he has discipled ten "Timothys" who are directing the work in almost military precision. Each of them in turn will be able to lead hundreds of additional workers who will have their own disciples.

As I sat down to write this chapter, I opened a letter from him telling of the missionary trip he just completed in Maharashtra state. Forty-two new churches were established there in twelve days. In another area populated by Mang tribals, fifty additional villages need full-time native evangelists to come and establish their new churches.

With his wife he set an apostolic pattern for their workers similar to that of the apostle Paul. On one evangelistic tour that lasted fifty-three days, he and his family traveled by bullock cart and foot into some of the most backward areas of the tribal districts of Orissa state. There, working in the intense heat among people whose life-style is so primitive that it can be described only as animalistic, he saw hundreds converted. Throughout the journey, demons were cast out, and miraculous physical healings took place daily. Thousands of the tribals — who are enslaved to idols and spirit-worship — heard the gospel eagerly.

In just one month he formed fifteen groups of converts into new churches and assigned native missionaries to stay behind and build them up in the faith.

Similar miraculous movements are starting in almost every state of India and throughout other nations of Asia.

In one area of India hundreds of villagers turned to the Lord when four of their pagan priests were miraculously saved.

Native missionary Jesu Das was horrified when he first visited the village and found no believers there. The people were all worshipping hundreds of different gods, and the four pagan priests controlled them through their witchcraft.

Stories were told of how these priests could kill people's cattle with witchcraft and destroy their crops. People were suddenly taken ill and died without explanation.

The destruction and bondage these people were living in is hard to imagine. Scars, decay and death were portrayed on their faces, because they were totally controlled by the powers of darkness.

When Jesu Das told them about Christ, it was the first time they ever heard that there was a God who did not require sacrifices and offerings to appease His anger.

As Jesu Das continued to preach in the marketplace, many

people came to know the Lord.

But the priests were outraged. They warned Jesu Das that if he did not leave the village, they would call on their gods to kill him, his wife and their children.

But Jesu Das did not leave. He continued to preach, and villagers continued to be saved.

Finally, after a few weeks, the witch doctors came to Jesu Das and asked him the secret of his power.

"This is the first time our power did not work," they told him. "After doing the 'pujas,' we asked the spirits to go and kill your family. But the spirits came back and told us they could not approach you or your family because you were always surrounded by fire.

"Then we called more powerful spirits to come after you — but they too returned, saying not only were you surrounded by fire, but angels were also around you all the time."

Jesu Das told them about Christ. The Holy Spirit convicted each of them of their sin of following demons and of the judgment to come.

With tears, they repented — renouncing their gods and idols — and received Jesus Christ as Lord.

As a result of their pagan priests following the Lord, hundreds of other villagers also were set free from sin and bondage.

In Thailand, where more than two hundred native missionaries with the Thai Ezra Team are pioneering village evangelism, one group personally shared their faith with 10,463 in two months. Of these, 171 gave their lives to Christ, and six new churches were formed.

Over one thousand came to Christ in the same reporting period. Remember, this great harvest is happening in a Buddhist nation that never has seen such results.

In the Philippines, where a native evangelistic team recently spent fifteen weeks reaching ten villages in Bataan, more than seventeen thousand were counseled for salvation. Another team with a traveling film ministry reported 44,548 conversions in 1983.

Documented reports like these come to us daily from native teams in almost every Asian nation. But I am convinced these are only the first few drops of revival rain. In order to make the necessary impact, we must send out hundreds of thousands more workers. We're no longer praying for the proverbial "showers of blessings" — we must see cloudbursts. I'm believing God for virtual thunderstorms of blessings in the days ahead.

How I became a part of this astonishing spiritual renewal in Asia is what this book is all about. And it all began with the prayers of a simple village mother.

2

O God,
Let One of My Boys Preach

Achiamma's eyes stung with salty tears. But they weren't from the cooking fire or the hot spices that wafted up from the pan. She realized time was short. Her six sons were growing beyond her influence. Yet not one showed signs of going into the gospel ministry.

Except for the youngest — little "Yohannachan" as I was known — every one of her children seemed destined for secular work. My brothers seemed content to live and work around our native village of Niranam in Kerala, South India.

"O God," she prayed in despair, "let just one of my boys preach!"

Like Hannah and so many other saintly mothers in the Bible, she had dedicated her children to the Lord. That morning, while preparing breakfast, she vowed to fast secretly until God called one of her sons into His service. Every Friday for the next three and a half years, she fasted. Her prayer was always the same.

But nothing happened. Finally, only I, scrawny and little — the baby of the family — was left. But there seemed little chance I would preach. I was so shy and timid I trembled when asked to recite in class. Although I had stood up in an evangelistic meeting at age eight, I kept my faith mostly to myself.

In fact, I had turned into the village's youngest recluse — a nonperson who avoided sports and school functions. I showed no leadership skills. I was comfortable on the edge of village and family life, a shadowy figure who moved in and out of the scene almost unnoticed.

Then, when I was sixteen, my mother's prayers were answered. A visiting gospel team from Operation Mobilization came to our church to present the challenge of faraway North India. My ninety-pound frame strained to catch every word as the team spoke and showed slides of the North.

They told of stonings and beatings they received while preaching Christ in the non-Christian villages of Rajasthan and Bihar. It stretched my imagination to visualize the hot arid plains of North India. Sheltered from contact with the rest of India by the high peaks of the Western Ghats, the lush coastal jungles of Kerala were all I knew of my homeland. The rest of India seemed an ocean away to the Malayalam-speaking people of the southwest coast, and I was no exception.

Besides the wildlife and fish that thrived in the surrounding rivers and tropical rain forests, the Malabar Coast had long nourished India's oldest Christian community. Christianity was one of India's oldest religions, because the flourishing sea trade with the Persian Gulf made it possible for St. Thomas to introduce Jesus Christ at nearby Cranagore in A.D. 52. Other Jews already were there, having arrived two hundred years earlier.

As the gospel team portrayed the desperately lost condition of the rest of the country — 500,000 villages without a gospel witness — I felt a strange sorrow for the lost. That day in my heart I vowed to help bring the good news of Jesus Christ to those strange and mysterious states to the North. At the challenge to "forsake all and follow Christ" I somewhat rashly took the leap, agreeing to join the student group for a short summer crusade in unreached parts of North India.

So my decision to go into the ministry was largely because of my mother's faithful prayers. Although I still hadn't received what I later understood to be my real call from the Lord, my mother encouraged me to follow my heart in the matter. When I announced my decision, she wordlessly handed over twenty-five rupees — enough for my train ticket. I set off to apply to the mission's headquarters in Trivandrum.

There I got my first rebuff. Since I was underage, they at first refused to let me join the teams going north. But I was permitted to attend the annual training conference to be held in Bangalore, Karnataka.

At the conference I heard missionary statesman George Verwer for the first time. He challenged me as never before to commit myself to a life of breathtaking, radical discipleship. I was impressed how Verwer himself put the will of God for the lost world before career, family and self.

Alone that night in my bed, I argued with both God and my own conscience. By two o'clock in the morning, my pillow was wet with sweat and tears. I shook with fear. What if God would ask me to preach in the streets? How would I ever be able to stand up in public and speak? What if I were stoned and beaten?

I knew myself only too well. I could hardly bear to look a friend in the eye during a conversation, let alone speak publicly to hostile crowds on behalf of God. As I spoke the words, I realized that I was behaving as Moses did when he was called.

Suddenly, I felt that I was not alone in the room. A great sense of love and of my being loved filled the place. I felt the presence of God and fell on my knees beside the bed.

"Lord God," I gasped in surrender to His presence and will, "I'll give myself to speak for You — but help me to know that You're with me."

Then it was morning. I awoke to a world and people suddenly different. Walking outside, the Indian street scenes were the same as before: children running between the legs of people and cows, pigs and chickens wandering about, vendors with baskets of bright fruit and flowers on their heads. I loved them all with a supernatural unconditional love I'd never felt before. It was just as if God had removed my eyes and replaced them with His.

For the first time I was seeing people as the heavenly Father sees them — lost and needy but with potential to glorify and reflect Him.

I walked to the bus station. My eyes filled with tears of love. I knew that these people were all going to hell — and I knew that God didn't want them to go there. Suddenly I had such a burden for these masses that I had to stop and lean against a wall just to keep my balance.

So this was it. I knew I was feeling the burden of love God feels for the lost multitudes of India. His loving heart was pounding within mine, and I could hardly breathe. The tension was great. I paced back and forth restlessly to keep my knees from knocking in fright.

"Lord!" I cried. "If You want me to do something, say it, and give me courage."

Looking up from my prayer I saw a huge stone. I knew immediately I had to climb that stone and preach to the crowds in the bus station. Scrambling up, I felt a force like ten thousand volts of electricity shooting through my body.

I began by singing a simple children's chorus. It was all I knew. By the time I finished, a crowd stood at the foot of the rock. I had not prepared myself to speak, but all at once God took over and filled my mouth with words of His love. I preached the gospel to the poor as Jesus commanded His disciples to do. I saw myself fulfilling His mission in His power.

Suddenly I had superhuman boldness. As the authority and power of God flowed through me, words came out I never knew I had — and with a power clearly from above.

Others from the gospel teams stopped to listen. The question of my age and calling never came up again. That was 1966, and I continued moving with mobile evangelistic teams for the next seven years.

We traveled all over North India, never staying very long in any one village. Everywhere I would preach in the streets, while others distributed books and tracts. Occasionally, in smaller villages, we would witness from house to house.

Although I often would witness and join in the ministry, my

real heart was with open-air preaching. I knew that most people were illiterate and enjoyed listening to me passionately proclaim the Lord.

Using a "wordless flag" stitched together from strips of cloth, I was able to explain the gospel easily to illiterate villagers. The flag had four bars of color and in itself attracted many people to learn its meaning. The black bar of cloth represented our sinful hearts before Christ entered. The red bar, His cleansing blood. The white, our new hearts; and the yellow, our hope of walking the golden streets of heaven. From the back of diesel vans, beside bicycles and on foot, this simple banner made the good news of Christ clear to thousands.

And with the flag we often would sing the children's chorus:

> "My heart was black with sin,
>   until the Savior came in.
> His precious blood I know,
>   has washed me white as snow.
> And in His word I'm told
>   I'll walk the streets of gold.
> Oh wonderful, wonderful day,
>   He washed my sins away."

My urgent, overpowering love for the village people of India and the poor masses grew with the years. People even began to nickname me "Gandhi Man" after the father of modern India, Mahatma Gandhi. Like him, I realized without being told that if India was to be won, it would be by brown-skinned natives who loved the village people.

Even as I studied the Gospels, it became clear to me that Jesus understood the principle well. He avoided the major cities, the rich, the famous and the powerful. Rather than go to the elite centers of influence, He concentrated His ministry on the poor laboring class. To reach India and the other nations of Asia, all we have to do is reach the poor.

As I traveled, viewing the effects of pagan religions on India,

I realized that the masses of India are starving because they are slaves to sin. The battle against hunger and poverty is really a spiritual battle, not a physical or social one as secularists would have us believe.

The only weapon that will ever effectively win the war against disease, hunger, injustice and poverty in Asia is the gospel of Jesus Christ. To look into the sad eyes of a hungry child or see the wasted life of a drug addict is to see only the evidence of Satan's hold on this world. All bad things are his handiwork. He is the ultimate enemy of mankind, and he will do everything within his considerable power to kill and destroy human beings. Fighting this powerful enemy with physical weapons is like fighting an armored tank with stones.

I can never forget one of the more dramatic encounters we had with these demonic powers. It was a hot and unusually humid day in 1970. We were preaching in the northwestern state of Rajasthan — the "desert of kings."

As was our practice before a street meeting, my seven co-workers and I stood in a circle to sing and clap hands to the rhythm of Christian folk songs. A sizeable crowd gathered, and I began to speak in Hindi, the local language. Many heard the gospel for the first time and eagerly took our Gospels and tracts to read.

One young man came up to me and asked for a book to read. As I talked to him, I sensed in my spirit that this was a person hungry to know God. As we got ready to climb aboard our gospel van, he asked to join us.

As the van lurched forward, he cried and wailed. "I am a terrible sinner," he shrieked. "How can I sit among you?" With that he started to jump from the moving van. We held on to him and forced him to the floor to prevent injury.

That night he stayed at our base and the next morning joined us for the prayer meeting. While we were praising and interceding, we heard a sudden scream. Then we saw the young man lying on the ground, tongue lolling out of his mouth, his eyes rolled back.

As Christians in a pagan land, we knew immediately he was demon-possessed. We gathered around him and began taking authority over the forces of hell as they spoke through his mouth.

"We are seventy-four of us....For the past seven years we have made him walk barefoot all over India....He is ours...." They spoke on, blaspheming and cursing, challenging us and our authority.

But as three of us prayed, the demons could not keep their hold on the young man. They came out when we commanded them to leave in the name of Jesus.

Sundar John was delivered. He gave his life to Jesus and was baptized. Later, he went to Bible school for two years. Since then the Lord has enabled him to teach and preach to thousands of people about Christ. Several native Indian churches have started as a result of his remarkable ministry — all this from a man many people would have locked up in an insane asylum.

Today, Sundar John is continuing in fellowship with us as a native missionary evangelist. But there are literally millions of people like him in India — deceived by demons and enslaved to their horrible passions and lusts.

This is the kind of miracle that kept me going from village to village for those seven years of itinerant preaching. Our lives read like pages from the book of Acts. Most nights we slept between villages in roadside ditches, where we were relatively safe. Sleeping in non-Christian villages would expose us to many dangers. Our team always created a stir, and at times we even faced stonings and beatings.

We were persecuted, hated and despised. Yet we kept going, knowing that we were blazing a trail for the gospel in districts that never before had experienced an encounter with Christ.

One such village was Bhundi in Rajasthan. This was the first place I was beaten and stoned for preaching the gospel. Often literature was destroyed. It seemed that mobs always were on the watch for us, and six times our street meetings were broken up. Our team leaders began to work elsewhere, avoiding Bhundi as much as possible. Three years later, a new team of native missionaries moved into the area under different leadership and preached again at this busy crossroads town.

Almost as soon as they arrived, one man began tearing up literature and grabbed a nineteen-year-old missionary, Alex Sam, by the throat. Although beaten severely, Sam knelt in the street and prayed for the salvation of souls in that hateful city.

"Lord," he prayed, "I want to come back here and serve You in Bhundi. I'm willing to die here, but I want to come back and serve You in this place."

Many older Christian leaders advised him against his decision, but being determined, he went back and rented a small room. Shipments of literature arrived, and he preached in the face of many difficulties. Today fifty people meet in a small church there. Those who persecuted us at one time now worship the Lord Jesus, as was the case with the apostle Paul.

This is the kind of commitment and faith it takes to win North Indian villages to the Lord Jesus.

At another time we arrived in a town at daybreak to preach. But word already had gone ahead from the nearby village where we had preached the day before.

As we had morning tea in a roadside stall, the local militant leader approached me politely. In a low voice that betrayed little emotion, he spoke:

"Get on your truck and get out of town in five minutes or we'll burn it and you with it."

I knew he was serious. He was backed by a menacing crowd.

Although we did "shake the dust from our feet" that day, there is a church meeting in that same village today. In order to plant the gospel, risks must be taken.

For months at a time I traveled the dusty roads in the heat of the day and shivered through cold nights — suffering just as thousands of native missionaries are suffering today to bring the gospel to the lost.

In future years I would look back on those seven years of village evangelism as one of the greatest learning experiences of my life. We walked in Jesus' steps, incarnating and representing Him to masses of people who had never heard the gospel before.

3

If Only She Were an Indian

I was living a frenetic, busy life — too busy and thrilled with the work of the gospel to think much about the future. There always was another campaign just ahead. The mobile gospel teams I worked with — and often led — were just like family to me. I came almost to enjoy the gypsy life-style we lived, and the total abandonment to the cause of Christ that is demanded of an itinerant evangelist.

But I was about to reach a turning point. In 1971 I was invited to spend one month in Singapore at a new institute which had been started by John Haggai. It was still in the formative stages then — a place where Asian church leaders would be trained and challenged to witness for Christ.

With Haggai was another of the great men of our times, Bob Pierce, founder of World Vision. My encounters with these men would eventually change the direction of my life, and their words were to haunt me for years to come.

When I met Haggai, I knew he believed in me instantly. I sensed he was not afraid for me to reach my full potential — that he wanted me to dream great dreams and accomplish God's very best for my life. Unlike so many Christian leaders from the West, there was nothing in Haggai that tried to hold me back or keep me in "my place."

He was the first person who made me believe that nothing is

impossible with God. He was full of stories. In them all, Christians were overcomers and giants — men and women who received a vision from God and refused to let go of it. Diligence to your calling was a virtue to be highly prized.

In both Pierce and Haggai I found men who refused to accept impossibilities. The normal boundaries accepted by others didn't exist for them. Here were men who saw everything in global terms and from God's perspective. I was walking on dizzying heights, dreaming dreams and thinking thoughts I'd never allowed myself to entertain in the past.

These were men who refused to accept sin. If the world was not evangelized, why not? If people were hungry, what could we do about it? These men didn't think like Hindus — they refused to accept the world as it was. And I discovered that they both were willing to accept personal responsibility to become change agents.

Pierce prayed like no man I had ever met. One of his prayers is still a regular part of my devotional life: "O loving God, break my heart with the things that break the heart of Jesus."

He told a story once that I have never forgotten. Early in his ministry he had been a part of the Billy Graham Evangelistic Team. Unlike the others, he seemed to have no outstanding public gift, and that troubled him. Finally, he prayed a prayer that eventually led him to Korea and the founding of World Vision:

> O living God, I cannot preach like Billy Graham. I cannot sing like Cliff Barrows. But, Lord — if there's something You want someone to do and they won't do it — then tell me. I promise I'll do it with all my heart, with everything I have in my power and in the best way I know how. Amen.

It was that servant spirit which led Bob Pierce to start World Vision on every continent and in every nation of Asia. Millions were touched in the two decades of his Asian ministry.

Toward the end of my month with them, John Haggai challenged me into the most painful introspection I have ever experienced. I know now it implanted a restlessness in me that would last for years.

It eventually would cause me to leave India to search abroad for God's ultimate will in my life.

Haggai's challenge seemed simple at first. He wanted me to go to my room and write down — in one sentence — the single most important thing I was going to do with the rest of my life.

He stipulated that it could not be self-centered or worldly in nature. And one more thing — it had to bring glory to God.

I went to my room to write that one sentence. But the paper remained blank for hours and days. I left the conference with the question still ringing in my ears.

For years I would hear the words of John Haggai, "One thing...by God's grace you have to do one thing." Disturbed that I might not be reaching my full potential in Christ, I began at that conference to re-evaluate every part of my life-style and ministry. Nothing changed right away, but I started the process of asking, seeking and knocking in prayer. I knew I had to find and submit to the specific will of God for my life.

I left Singapore newly liberated to think of myself in terms of an individual for the first time. Up until that time — like most Asians — I always had viewed myself as part of a group, either my family or a gospel team. Although I had no idea what special work God would have for me as an individual, I began thinking of doing my "personal best" for Him.

The seeds for future change had been planted, and nothing could stop the approaching storms in my life.

While my greatest passion was still for the unreached villages of the North, I now was traveling all over India.

On one of these speaking trips in 1973, I was invited to teach at the spring Operation Mobilization training conference in Madras. That was where I first saw the attractive German girl.

As a student in one of my classes, she impressed me with the simplicity of her faith. Soon I found myself thinking that if she were an Indian, she would be the kind of woman I would like to marry some day.

Once, when our eyes met, we held each other's gaze for a brief, extra moment, until I self-consciously broke the spell and quickly fled the room. I was uncomfortable in such male-female encounters. In our culture, single people seldom speak to each other. Even in church and on gospel teams, the sexes are kept strictly separate.

Certain that I would never again see her, I pushed the thought of the attractive German girl from my mind. But marriage was on my mind. I had made a list of the six qualities I most wanted in a wife and frequently prayed for the right choice to be made for me.

Of course, in India, all marriages are arranged by the parents, and I would have to rely on their judgment in selecting the right person for my life partner. I wondered where my parents would find a wife who was willing to share my mobile life-style and commitment to the work of the gospel. But as the conference ended, plans for the summer outreach soon crowded out these thoughts.

That summer, along with a few co-workers, I returned to all the places we had visited during the last few years in the state of Punjab. I had been in and out of the state many times and was eager to see the fruit of our evangelism there.

The breadbasket of India, the Punjab is one of the richest agricultural areas in the world. Just as the flat plains of Kansas supply most of America's wheat, the Punjab produces most of the wheat and other grains of India. Its population of fifteen million is dominated by turbaned Sikhs, a fiercely independent and hardworking people who have always been a caste of warriors.

Before the partition of India and Pakistan, the state also had a huge Muslim population. It remains one of the least evangelized and most neglected areas of the world.

We had trucked and street-preached our way through hundreds of towns and villages in this state over the previous two years. Although British missionaries had founded many hospitals and schools in the state, very few congregations of believers now existed. The intensely nationalistic Sikhs stubbornly refused to consider Christianity, since they closely associated it with British colonialism.

I traveled with a good-sized team of men. A separate women's team also was assigned to the state, working out of Jullundur.

On my way north to link up with the men's team I would lead, I stopped in at the North India headquarters in New Delhi.

To my surprise there she was again — the German girl. This time she was dressed in a sari, one of the most popular forms of our national dress. I learned she also had been assigned to work in Punjab for the summer with the women's team.

The local director asked me to escort her northward as far as Jullundur, and so we rode in the same van. I learned her name was Gisela, and the more I saw of her the more enchanted I became.

She ate the food and drank the water and unconsciously followed all the rules of our culture.

The little conversation we had focused on spiritual things and the lost villages of India. I soon realized I had finally found a soul mate who shared my vision and calling.

Romantic love, for most Indians, is something you read about only in storybooks. Daring cinema films, while they frequently deal with the concept, are careful to end the film in a proper Indian manner.

So I was faced with the big problem of communicating my forbidden and impossible love. I said nothing to Gisela, of course. But something in her eyes told me we both understood. Could God be bringing us together?

In a few hours we would be separated again, and I reminded myself I had other things to do. Besides, I thought, at the end of the summer she'll be flying to Germany, and I'll probably never see her again.

Throughout the summer, surprisingly, our paths did cross again. Each time I felt my love grow stronger. Then I tentatively took a chance at expressing my love with a letter.

Meanwhile, the Punjab survey broke my heart. In village after village I found that our literature and preaching appeared to have little lasting impact. I still hadn't learned the secret of making disciples and planting churches. So the fruit had not remained. Most of the villages we visited appeared just as illiterate, idolatrous and demon-controlled as ever. The people still were locked in disease, poverty and suffering. The gospel, it seemed to me, hadn't taken root.

Finally, in one town I felt such deep despair I literally sat down on a curb and sobbed. I wept the bitter tears that only a child can cry.

"Your work is for nothing," taunted a demon in my ear. "Your words are rolling off these people like water off a duck's back!"

Without realizing I was burning out — or what was happening to me spiritually — I fell into listlessness. Like Jonah and Elijah, I was too tired to go on. I could see only one thing. The fruit of my work wasn't remaining. More than ever before, I needed time to reassess my ministry.

My co-leaders, alarmed at my personal crisis and aware that something was deeply wrong, insisted I take a month off to recoup. I went to Bombay for that month.

While there, I corresponded with Gisela. She had, in the meantime, returned to Germany. I finally decided I would take two years off from the work to study and make some life choices about my ministry and possible marriage.

I began writing letters abroad and became interested in the possibility of attending a Bible school in England. I also had invitations to speak in churches in Germany.

In December I bought an air ticket out of India. I would be in Europe for Christmas with Gisela's family.

During the next month I got the first tremors of what soon would become an earthquake-size case of culture shock.

As the snow fell, it was obvious to everyone I soon would have to buy a winter coat and boots — obvious, that is, to everyone except me. One look at the price tags sent me into deep trauma. For the cost of my coat and boots in Germany, I could have lived comfortably for months back in India.

And living by faith was hard for my future in-laws to accept. Here was this penniless street preacher from India, without a single dollar of his own, insisting he was going to school but he didn't know where, and asking to marry their daughter.

One by one the miracles occurred, though, and God met every need.

First, a letter arrived from E.A. Gresham, a total stranger from Dallas, Texas, who was then regional director of the Fellowship of Christian Athletes. He had heard about me from a Scottish friend and invited me to come to the United States for two years of study at what was then the Criswell Bible Institute in Dallas. I replied positively and booked myself on a low-cost charter flight to New York with the last money I had. This flight, it turned out, also was to become a miracle.

Not knowing I needed a special student visa, I bought the ticket without the chance for refund. If I missed the flight, I would lose both my seat and the ticket.

Praying with my last ounce of faith, I asked God to intervene and somehow get the paperwork for the visa. As I prayed, a friend in Dallas, Texas, was strangely moved to get out of his car, go back to the office and complete the paperwork. Later, he testified of a strange urge from God compelling him to complete the paperwork and personally take it to the post office. In a continuous series of divinely arranged "coincidences," the forms arrived within hours of the deadline.

Before leaving for America, Gisela and I became engaged. I would go on to seminary alone, however. We had no idea when we would see each other again.

4

I Walked
in a Daze

As I changed planes for Dallas at JFK International in New York, I was overcome at the sights and sounds around me. Overseas you hear stories about the affluence and prosperity of America, but until you see it with your own eyes, the stories seem like fairy tales.

But Americans are more than just unaware of their affluence — they almost seem to despise it at times. Finding a lounge chair, I stared in amazement at how they treated their beautiful clothes and shoes. The richness of the fabrics and colors was beyond anything I had ever seen. As I would discover again and again, this is a nation that routinely takes its astonishing wealth for granted.

As I would do many times — almost daily — in the weeks ahead, I compared their clothing to that of the native missionary evangelists whom I had left only a few weeks before. Many of them walk barefoot between villages or work in flimsy sandals. Their threadbare cotton clothing would not be acceptable as cleaning rags in the United States. Then I discovered most Americans have closets full of clothing they wear only occasionally — and I remembered the years I traveled and worked with only the clothes on my back. I had lived the normal life-style of most village evangelists.

Economist Robert Heilbroner describes the luxuries a typical

American family would have to surrender if they lived among the
one billion hungry people in the Third World:

> We begin by invading the house of our imaginary
> American family to strip it of its furniture. Every-
> thing goes: beds, chairs, tables, television sets,
> lamps. We will leave the family with a few old
> blankets, a kitchen table, a wooden chair. Along with
> the bureaus go the clothes. Each member of the
> family may keep in his 'wardrobe' his oldest suit or
> dress, a shirt or blouse. We will permit a pair of shoes
> for the head of the family, but none for the wife or
> children.
>
> We move to the kitchen. The appliances have
> already been taken out, so we turn to the cup-
> boards...the box of matches may stay, a small bag of
> flour, some sugar and salt. A few moldy potatoes,
> already in the garbage can, must be rescued, for they
> will provide much of tonight's meal. We will leave
> a handful of onions, and a dish of dried beans. All
> the rest we take away: the meat, the fresh vegetables,
> the canned goods, the crackers, the candy.
>
> Now we have stripped the house: the bathroom
> has been dismantled, the running water shut off, the
> electric wires taken out. Next we take away the
> house. The family can move to the toolshed.... Com-
> munications must go next. No more newspapers,
> magazines, books — not that they are missed, since
> we must take away our family's literacy as well.
> Instead, in our shantytown we will allow one ra-
> dio....
>
> Now government services must go next. No
> more postmen, no more firemen. There is a school,
> but it is three miles away and consists of two class-
> rooms....There are, of course, no hospitals or doctors
> nearby. The nearest clinic is ten miles away and is

tended by a midwife. It can be reached by bicycle, provided the family has a bicycle, which is unlikely....

Finally, money. We will allow our family a cash hoard of five dollars. This will prevent our breadwinner from experiencing the tragedy of an Iranian peasant who went blind because he could not raise the $3.94 which he mistakenly thought he needed to receive admission to a hospital where he could have been cured.[1]

This is an accurate description of the life-style and world from which I came. From the moment I touched foot on American soil, I walked in an unbelieving daze. How can two so different economies co-exist simultaneously on the earth? Everything was so overpowering and confusing to me at first. Not only did I have to learn the simplest procedures — like using the pay telephones and making change — but as a sensitive Christian, I found myself constantly making spiritual evaluations of everything I saw.

As the days passed into weeks, I began with alarm to understand how misplaced are the spiritual values of most Western believers. Sad to say, it appeared to me that for the most part they had absorbed the same humanistic and materialistic values that dominated the secular culture. Almost immediately I sensed an awesome judgment was hanging over the United States — and that I had to warn God's people that He was not going to lavish this abundance on them forever. But the message was still not formed in my heart, and it would be many years before I would feel the anointing and courage to speak out against such sin.

Meanwhile, in Texas, a land that in many ways epitomizes America, I reeled with shock at the most common things. My hosts eagerly pointed out what they considered their greatest achievements. I nodded with politeness as they showed me their huge churches, high-rise buildings and universities. But these didn't impress me very much. After all, I had seen the Golden Temple in Amritsar, the Taj Mahal, the Palaces of Jhans, the university of Baroda in Gujarat.

But what impresses visitors from the Third World are the simple things that Americans take for granted: fresh water available twenty-four hours a day, unlimited electrical power, telephones that work and a most remarkable network of paved roads. In India, the water, electricity, telephones and transportation operate erratically — if at all. Communication is a nightmare. We must wait days for long-distance calls to go through. At the time, we still had no television in India, but my American hosts seemed to have TV sets in every room — and operating day and night. This ever-present blast of media also disturbed me. For some reason, Americans seemed to have a need to surround themselves with noise all the time. Even in their cars, I noticed the radios ran when no one was listening.

Why do they always have to be either entertained or entertaining? I wondered. It was as if they were trying to escape from a guilt they hadn't yet defined or even identified.

Perhaps it was because I still weighed less than 110 pounds, but I was constantly aware of how large — and overweight — most Americans seemed to be. There is a reason why Americans need big cars, big homes and large furniture. They are big people. This came home vividly to me when I went to buy clothes. Like so many other Asian students, I had to go to the youth departments in the stores — adult sizes were just too large.

I was amazed at how important eating, drinking, smoking and even drug use were in the Western life-style. Even among Christians, food was a major part of fellowship events.

This, of course, is not bad in itself. "Love feasts" were an important part of the New Testament church life. But eating can be taken to extremes. One of the ironies of this is the relatively small price North Americans pay for food. One study showed that in the United States only 17 percent of disposable income is spent on food. In India it is 67 percent. When you have $10,000 to spend, that 17 percent works out to a comfortable $1,700. For the Indian family earning $200, 67 percent is $134. This is the kind of reality I had lived with every day, but Americans have real

47

trouble thinking in these terms.

Often I would speak at a church, and the people would apparently be quite moved as I told of the suffering and needs of the native evangelists. They usually would take an offering and present me with a check. At first, this seemed like a great amount of money. Then with their usual hospitality, I would be invited to eat with the leaders following the meeting. To my horror the cost of the food and "fellowship" would frequently be more than the money they had just given to missions. To my amazement I found that American families routinely eat enough meat at one meal to feed an Asian family for a week. No one ever seemed to notice this but me, and slowly I realized they just hadn't heard the meaning of my message. They were simply incapable of understanding the enormous needs overseas.

Even today I sometimes cannot freely order food when traveling in the United States. I look at the costs and realize how far the same amount of money will go in India, Burma or the Philippines. Suddenly I'm not quite as hungry as I was before.

Many native missionaries and their families experience days without food — not because they are fasting voluntarily — but because they don't have money to buy rice. This occurs especially when they start new work in villages where there are no Christians.

Remembering the heartbreaking suffering of the native brethren, I sometimes would refuse to eat the desserts so often served to me. I'm sure this made no difference in supplying food to hungry families, but I couldn't bear to take pleasure in eating while Christian workers in Asia were going hungry. The need became real to me through the ministry of Brother Moses Paulose, who is today one of the native missionaries we sponsor.

There are thousands of islands and endless miles of coastal backwaters in Asia. Millions of poor, uneducated fisherfolk live along these coastlines. Their homes usually are small huts made of leaves and their life-styles are simple — hard work and little pleasure.

These fishermen and their families are some of the most

unreached people in the world. Hardly any mission work ever has been done among them. But God called Paulose and his family to take the gospel to the unreached fishing villages of Tamil Nadu on the East Coast of India.

I remember visiting his family. One of the first things he discovered when he began visiting the villages was that the literacy rate was so low he could not use tracts or printed materials effectively. So he decided to use slides. All that stood in his way was the fact that he had no projector or money to purchase one.

In order to buy the projector, he made repeated trips to a hospital where he sold his blood until he had the money he needed.

It was exciting to see the crowds his slide projector attracted. As soon as he began to put up the white sheet which served as a screen, thousands of adults and children gathered along the beach. Mrs. Paulose sang gospel songs over a loudspeaker powered by a car battery, and their five-year-old son quoted Bible verses to passersby.

When the sun had set, Brother Paulose began his slide/preaching presentation. For several hours, thousands sat in the sand, listening to the gospel message while the sea murmured in the background. When we finally packed to leave, I had to walk carefully to avoid stepping on the hundreds of children sleeping on the sand.

But the tragedy behind all this was the secret starvation he and his family faced. Once I heard his long-suffering wife comforting the children and urging them to drink water from a baby bottle in order to hold off the pangs of hunger. There wasn't enough money in the house for milk.

Ashamed to let the non-Christian neighbors know he was without food, he would keep the windows and doors in his one-room rented house closed so they couldn't hear the cries of his four hungry children.

On another occasion, one of his malnourished children fell asleep in school because he was so weak from hunger. "I am ashamed to tell the teacher or our neighbors," he told me. "Only

God, our children, and my wife and I know the real story. We have no complaints or even unhappiness. We're joyfully and totally content in our service of the Lord. It is a privilege to be counted worthy to suffer for His sake...."

Even when the teacher punished his children for lack of attention in class, Paulose would not tell his secret suffering and bring shame on the name of Christ. Fortunately, in this case, we were able to send immediate support to him, thanks to the help of generous American Christians. But for too many others, the story does not end as happily.

Is it God's fault that men like Brother Paulose are going hungry? I don't think so. God has provided more than enough money to meet his needs and all the needs of the Third World. *The needed money is in the highly developed nations of the West.* North American Christians alone, without much sacrifice, can meet all the needs of the churches in the Third World.

A friend in Dallas recently pointed out a new church building costing $37 million. While this thought was still exploding in my mind, he pointed out another $7-million church building going up less than a minute away.

These extravagant buildings are insanity from a Third World perspective. The $37 million spent on one new building here could build nearly seventy-five hundred average-sized churches in India. The same $37 million would be enough to guarantee the evangelization of a whole state — or even some of the smaller countries of Asia.

But I rarely spoke out on these subjects. I realized I was a guest. The Americans who had built these buildings had also built the school I was now attending, and they were paying my tuition to attend. It amazed me, though, that these buildings have been constructed to worship Jesus, who said, "The foxes have holes, and the birds of the air have nests; but the Son of Man hath not where to lay his head" (Matt. 8:20).

In Asia today, Christ is still wandering homeless. He is looking for a place to lay His head, but in temples "not made with human hands." Our newborn Christians usually meet in their homes. In non-Christian communities, it is often impossible to rent church facilities. Instead of hindering church growth and evangelism, I have found this often increases our impact on the community.

There is such an emphasis on church buildings that we sometimes forget that the church is the people — not the place where the people meet.

But God has not called me to fight against church building programs. I think what troubles me much more than the waste is that these efforts represent a worldly mind-set.

Why can't we at least vow to spend a simple tithe of what we use for ourselves in the cause of world evangelism? If churches in the United States alone had made this commitment in 1986, there would have been $4.8 billion available to gospel outreach!

And what's more, if we had used these funds to support native missions, we could have fielded an army of evangelists the size of a major city.

5

A Nation Asleep in Bondage

Religion, I discovered, is a multi-billion dollar business in the United States. Entering churches, I was astonished at the carpeting, furnishings, air conditioning and ornamentation. Many churches have gymnasiums and fellowships that cater to a busy schedule of activities having little or nothing to do with Christ.

The orchestras, choirs, "special" music — and sometimes even the preaching — seemed to me more like entertainment than worship.

Many North American Christians live isolated from reality — not only from the needs of the poor overseas, but even from the poor in their own cities. Amidst all the affluence, there are millions of terribly poor people. But Christians have moved into the suburbs and left these people living in the inner city. I found that believers are ready to get involved in almost any activity which looks spiritual but allows them to escape their responsibility to the gospel.

For example, one morning I picked up a popular Christian magazine. There were many interesting articles, stories and reports from all over the world — most written by famous Christian leaders in the West.

Then I noticed what this magazine offered me as a Christian. There were ads for twenty-one Christian colleges, seminaries and correspondence courses; five different English translations of the

Bible; seven conferences and retreats; five new Christian films; nineteen commentaries and devotional books; seven Christian health or diet programs; five fund-raising services.

But that wasn't all. There were many little ads for all kinds of products and services: counseling, chaplaincy services, writing courses, church steeples, choir robes, wall crosses, baptistries and water heaters, T-shirts, records, tapes, adoption agencies, tracts, poems, gifts, book clubs and pen pals.

It was all rather impressive. Probably none of these things is wrong in itself, but it bothered me that one nation should have such spiritual luxury while forty thousand people were dying in my homeland every day without hearing the gospel even once.

In Christian bookstores I found varieties of products beyond my ability to imagine. If the affluence of America impressed me, the affluence of Christians impressed me even more.

The United States has about five thousand Christian book and gift stores — and many secular stores also carry religious books. All this while more than four thousand of the world's nearly six thousand five hundred languages are still without a single portion of the Bible published in their own language. In his book *My Billion Bible Dream*, Rochunga Pudaite says, "Eighty-five percent of all Bibles printed today are in English for the nine percent of the world who read English. Eighty percent of the world's people have never owned a Bible while Americans have an average of four in every household."[1]

Besides books, there are well over a thousand Christian magazines and newspapers. Christian radio and television are heard twenty-four hours a day around the clock in almost every part of the country. Over fifteen hundred Christian radio stations broadcast the gospel full time, while most countries don't even have their first Christian radio station. Nearly two thousand radio and TV programs are produced for Christians in the United States, but fewer than four hundred are produced for use overseas.

The saddest observation I can make about most of the religious communication activity of the Western world is this: *Little, if any, of this media is designed to reach unbelievers. Almost all is entertainment for the saints.*

The United States is blessed with over one million full-time Christian workers, or one full-time religious leader for every 230 people in the nation. What a difference this is from the rest of the world, where 2.7 billion people have still to hear the gospel once. Among the unreached or "hidden peoples" there is only one missionary working for every 500,000 people. These are the masses for whom Christ wept and died. They have yet to hear the gospel even once.

There are still 16,000 distinct cultural groups in the world without a single church among them to preach the gospel, while America has between 400,000 and 450,000 congregations or groups.[2]

One of the most impressive blessings in America is religious liberty. Not only do Christians have access to radio and television, unheard of in most nations of Asia, but they are also free to hold meetings, convert and evangelize, and print literature. Donations to Christian organizations are tax-exempt. How different this is from many Asian nations where government persecution of Christians is common and often legal.

Such was the case in Nepal, where until recently it was illegal to change one's religion or to influence others to change their religion. According to the law, you were to remain forever in the religion into which you were born. Christians often faced prison there for their faith.

Perhaps the most famous Nepali prisoner is Brother P—, known as the "Apostle to Nepal." This native missionary served time in fourteen different prisons between 1960 and 1975. He spent ten out of those fifteen years suffering torture and ridicule for preaching the gospel to his people.

His ordeal began when he baptized nine new believers and was arrested for doing so. The new converts, five men and four women, also were arrested, and each was sentenced to a year in prison. P— was sentenced to serve six years for influencing them.

Nepali prisons are typically Asian — literally dungeons of death. About twenty-five or thirty people are jammed into one small room with no ventilation or sanitation. The smell is so bad that newcomers often pass out in less than half an hour.

The place was crawling with lice and cockroaches. Prisoners slept on dirt floors. Rats and mice gnawed on fingers and toes during the night. In the winter there was no heat; in summer no ventilation.

For food, the prisoners were allowed one cup of rice each day, but they had to build a fire on the ground to cook it. The room was constantly filled with smoke since there was no chimney. On that inadequate diet, most prisoners became seriously ill, and the stench of vomit was added to the other putrefying odors. Yet, miraculously, none of the Christians was sick for even one day during the entire year.

After serving their one-year sentences, the nine new believers were released. Then the authorities decided to break P — . They took his Bible away from him, chained him hand and foot, then forced him through a low doorway into a tiny cubicle previously used to store bodies of dead prisoners until relatives came to claim them.

In the damp darkness, the jailer predicted his sanity would not last more than a few days. The room was so small he could not stand up or even stretch out on the floor. He could not build a fire to cook, so other prisoners slipped food under the door to keep him alive.

Lice ate away his underwear, but he could not scratch because of the chains, which soon cut his wrists and ankles to the bone. It was winter, and he nearly froze to death several times.

He could not tell day from night, but as he closed his eyes, God let him see the pages of the New Testament. Although his Bible had been taken away, he was still able to read it in total darkness. It sustained him as he endured the terrible torture. For three months he was not allowed to speak to another human being.

P— was transferred to many other prisons. In each, he continually shared his faith with both guards and prisoners.

Although P— is constantly in and out of prisons, he has refused to form secret churches. "How can a Christian keep silent?" he asks. "How can a church go underground? Jesus died openly for us. He did not try to hide on the way to the cross. We also must speak out boldly for Him regardless of the consequences."

Coming from India, where I was beaten and stoned for my faith, I know what it is to be a persecuted minority in my own country. When I set foot on Western soil, I could sense a spirit of religious liberty. North Americans have never known the fear of persecution. Nothing seems impossible to them. Christians here go about their affairs without giving a thought to the possibility of persecution.

With all these blessings, the abundance in both spiritual and material things, affluence unsurpassed by any nation on earth, with a totally unfettered church, I expected to see a much bolder witness. God's grace obviously has been poured out on nation and church in a way no other people ever have experienced.

From India, I always had looked to America as a fortress of Christianity. Instead I found a church in spiritual decline.

American believers are still the leading givers to missions, but this appeared due more to historical accident than the deep-set conviction I expected to find. As I spoke in churches and met average Christians, I discovered they had terrible misconceptions about the missionary mandate of the church. In church meetings — as I listened to the questions of my hosts and heard their comments about the Third World — my heart would almost burst with pain.

These people, I knew, were capable of so much more. They were dying spiritually, but I knew God wanted to give them life again. He wanted His church to recover its moral mandate and sense of mission.

I didn't yet know how. I didn't know when. But I knew one thing: *God did not shower such great blessing on this nation for the Christians to live in extravagance, in self-indulgence and in spiritual weakness.*

By faith, I could see a revival coming — the body of Christ rediscovering the power of the gospel and their obligation to it.

But for the time being, all I could do was sense how wrong the situation was — and pray. God had not given me the words to articulate what I was seeing — or a platform from which to speak. Instead He still had some important lessons to teach me, and I was to learn them in an alien land far from my beloved India.

6

What Are You Doing Here?

The Bible says "some plant" and "others water." The living God now took me halfway around the world to teach me about watering. Before He could trust me again with the planting, I had to learn the lesson I'd been avoiding in India — *the importance of the local church in God's master plan for world evangelism.*

It really started through one of those strange coincidences — a divine appointment that only a sovereign God could engineer.

By now I was a busy divinity student in Dallas at the Criswell Bible Institute, intently soaking up every one of my classes. Thanks to the scholarship that God had so miraculously provided, I was able to dig into God's Word as never before. For the first time I was doing formal, in-depth study, and the Bible was revealing many of its secrets to me.

After my first term, Gisela and I were married, and she joined me in Dallas at the beginning of the next school term, October 1974. Except for preaching engagements and opportunities to share about Asia on weekends, I was fully absorbed in my studies and establishing our new home.

One weekend a fellow student invited me to fill the pulpit at a little church he was pastoring in Dallas. Although it was an American congregation, there were many native American Indians in fellowship.

Gisela was especially thrilled because through much of her childhood, she had prayed to be a missionary to "Red Indians on the Great Plains of America." While other schoolgirls dreamed of marriage and a Prince Charming, she was praying about doing ministry work among Native Americans. Much to my surprise, I found she had collected and read more than a hundred books about the tribal life and history of American Indians.

Strangely challenged and burdened for this little congregation, I preached my heart out. Never once did I mention my vision and burden for Asia. Instead I expounded Scripture verse by verse. A great love whelmed up in me for these people.

Although I didn't know it, my pastor friend turned in his resignation the same day. The deacons invited me to come back the next week and the next. God gave me a supernatural love for these people, and they loved us back.

Late that month the church board invited me to become the pastor, at the age of twenty-three. When Gisela and I accepted the call, I instantly found myself carrying a burden for these people twenty-four hours a day.

More than once I shamefacedly remembered how I had despised pastors and their problems back in India. Now that I was patching up relationships, healing wounded spirits and holding a group together, I started to see things in a wholly different light.

Some of the problems God's people face are the same worldwide, so I preached against sin and for holy living. Other problems (such as divorce, an epidemic in the West but almost unheard of in India) I was completely unprepared to handle.

Although my weight had increased to 106 pounds, I still nearly collapsed when I attempted to baptize a 250-pound convert! We had regular water baptisms and people came to Christ continually. We were a growing, soul-winning church with a hectic round of meetings that went six nights a week.

Besides preaching twice on Sunday and at the Wednesday night prayer meetings, I taught home Bible studies and the adult Sunday school class.

The days passed quickly into months. When I wasn't in

classes, I was with my people. We learned to visit in homes, call on the sick in hospitals, marry and bury. Gisela and I were involved in the lives of our people day and night. I gave myself to them with the same abandonment that characterized my village preaching in North India.

Since we had several Indian tribal groups represented in the congregation as well as "anglos," we soon found we were having much more than a two-way, cross-cultural experience. We actually were ministering to several different cultures simultaneously.

The "staying power" and disciple-making were what my ministry in North India had lacked. I saw why I had failed in the Punjab. It isn't enough to hold evangelistic crusades and bring people to Christ. Someone has to stay behind and nurture the new believers into maturity.

Now God was showing me the answer to my prayers back in the Punjab. When I sat on that curb in Ferozpur and wept out the question, Where is the fruit? I was really asking, Where is the church? Now called to be a pastor, I was experiencing the process of how fruit is preserved. This, I understood at last, is what my work back in India had lacked.

For the first time I began to understand the goal of all mission work. It is the "perfecting" of the saints into sanctified, committed disciples of Christ. Jesus commanded us to go to all the nations, baptizing them and teaching them to obey all the things He had revealed. The gospel-team ministry I had led in India was going, but we weren't staying to do the teaching.

The church — a group of believers — is God's ordained place for the discipleship process to take place. God's Plan A for the redemption of the world is the church, and He has no Plan B. The Bible says that Jesus loved the church. He laid down His life for her — His bride. He is coming back for a community of believers who have been made spotless.

As I went through the process of shepherding a local congregation, the Lord revealed to me that the same qualities are needed in native missionary evangelists. Now I knew what kind of men and women would be needed to reach the hidden peoples of Asia.

In my imagination I saw these same discipleship concepts being implanted in India and throughout Asia. Like the early Methodist circuit riders who planted churches on the American frontier, I could see our evangelists adding church planting to their evangelistic efforts.

But even as the concept captured me, I realized it would take an army of people — an army of God — to accomplish this task. In India alone, 500,000 villages are without a gospel witness. And then there are China, Southeast Asia and the islands. I could see we would easily need a million workers to finish the task.

But this was an idea too big for me to accept, so I pushed these thoughts from my mind. After all, I reasoned to myself, God has called me to this little church here in Dallas. I was getting very comfortable where I was. The church supported us well.

Didn't God miraculously bring us here? I argued with my conscience. God was blessing my ministry. Our first baby was on the way. I had begun to accept the Western way of life as my own, complete with a house, automobile, credit cards, insurance policies and bank accounts.

My formal schooling continued as I prepared to settle into building up the church. But my peace about staying in Dallas was slipping away.

By the end of 1976 and early in 1977, I heard an accusing voice every time I stood in the pulpit: What are you doing here? While you preach to an affluent American congregation, millions are going to hell in Asia. Have you forgotten your people?

A terrible inner conflict developed. I wasn't able to recognize the voice. Was it God? Was it my own conscience? Was it demonic? In desperation, I decided to wait upon God for His plan. I had said we would go anywhere, do anything. But we had to hear definitely from God. I just couldn't go on working with that tormenting voice.

Finally I announced to the church that I was praying, and I asked them to join with me in seeking the will of God for our future ministry.

"I seem to have no peace," I admitted to them, "about either staying in the United States or returning to India." *What is God really trying to say to me?*

As I prayed and fasted, God revealed Himself to me in a vision. It came back several times before I understood the revelation.

Many faces would appear before me — the faces of Asian men and their families. They weren't all Indians. They were from many lands. They were holy men and women, with a look of dedication on their faces. Gradually, I understood who these people were. It was like an image of the army of God that is now being raised up to take the gospel to every part of Asia.

Then the Lord spoke to me: "They cannot speak what you will speak. They will not go where you will go. You are called to be their servant. You must go where I will send you on their behalf. You are called to be their servant."

As lightning floods the sky in a storm, my whole life passed before me in that instant. I had never spoken English until I was sixteen, yet now I was ministering in this strange language. I had never worn shoes before I was seventeen. I was born and raised in a jungle village. Suddenly I realized I had nothing to be proud of; it wasn't my talents or skills that had brought me to America. My coming here was an act of God's sovereign will. He wanted me to cross cultures, to marry a German wife and live in an alien land. All this preparation was to give me the experiences I would need to serve in a new missionary movement.

"I have led you to this point," said God. "Your lifetime call is to be the servant of the unknown brethren — men whom I have called out and scattered among the villages of Asia."

Every Christian needs to know God's calling. We are commanded to know the will of God for our lives (see Eph. 5:17). I was as excited as a child with a new toy.

Knowing that at last I had found my life's work, I eagerly rushed to share my new vision with my church leaders and executives of missionary societies. To my utter bewilderment, God seemed to have forgotten to tell anyone but me.

My friends thought I was crazy. Mission leaders questioned either my integrity or my qualifications — and sometimes both.

Church leaders whom I trusted and respected wrapped fatherly arms around my shoulders and counseled me against undue emotionalism.

Suddenly, through a simple announcement, I found myself alone — under attack and forced to defend myself. I was aware that following the call of Jesus always involves some degree of suffering and persecution. Now I knew that had I not waited for such a clear calling, I undoubtedly would have collapsed under those early storms of unbelief and doubt. But in my heart I remained convinced of my call — certain that God was initiating a new day in world missions. Still no one seemed to catch my enthusiasm.

Secretly I had prided myself on being a good speaker and salesman, but nothing I could do or say seemed to turn the tide of public opinion. While I was arguing that "new wine needed new wineskins," others could only ask, "Where is the new wine?"

My only comfort was Gisela. She had been with me in India, and she accepted the vision without question. In moments of discouragement, when even my faith wavered, she refused to allow us to let go of the vision. Rebuffed, but certain that we had heard God correctly, we planted the first seeds by ourselves.

I wrote to an old friend in India whom I'd known and trusted for years, asking him to help me select some needy native missionaries who already were doing outstanding work. I promised to come and meet them later, and we started planning a survey trip to seek out more qualified workers.

Slowly, from out of my church salary and Gisela's nursing pay, we sent the first few dollars to India.

I became compulsive. Soon I couldn't buy a hamburger or drink a cola without feeling guilty. We quietly sold off everything we could, pulled our savings out of the bank and cashed in my life insurance.

We realized we had fallen into the trap of materialism. In seminary we were required to take courses on practical matters. I still can remember how my professor solemnly instructed his class of young "preacher boys" to lay aside money every month for emergencies, purchase life insurance and build equity in a home.

But I couldn't find any of this in the New Testament commands of Christ. Why was it necessary to save our money in bank accounts when Jesus commanded us not to lay up treasures on this earth? The Lord began to speak to me about all of this.

"Haven't I commanded you to live by faith?" asked the Holy Spirit.

So Gisela and I conformed our lives literally to the New Testament commands of Christ regarding money and material possessions. I even traded in my late model car for a cheaper used one. The difference went straight to India. It was a joy to make these little sacrifices for the native brethren. I knew that it was the only way we could get the mission started.

In those early days, what kept me going was the assurance that there was no other way. Even if people didn't understand that we had to start a native missionary movement, I felt an obligation to the knowledge of God's call.

First, I knew Western missions never could get the job done. Since my own nation and many others were closed to outsiders, we had to turn to the native believers. Even if Western missionaries somehow were permitted back, the cost of sending them would be in the billions each year. Native evangelists could do the same for only a fraction of the cost.

I never told anyone that I eventually would need such huge sums of money. They already thought I was crazy for wanting to support eight or ten missionaries a month out of my own income. What would they think if I said I needed millions of dollars a year to field an army of God?

But I knew it was possible. Several Western missionary societies and charities already were dealing with annual budgets that size. I saw no reason why we couldn't do the same. But as logical as it all was in my mind, I had some bitter lessons to learn.

Giving birth to a new mission society was going to take much more energy and start-up capital than I ever could imagine. I had a lot to learn about America and the way things are done here. But

I didn't know anything about that yet. I just knew it had to be done.

With youthful zest, Gisela and I went to India to do our first field survey. We returned a month later, penniless but committed to organizing what eventually would become Gospel for Asia.

Soon after our return, I revealed my decision to the congregation. Reluctantly we cut the cords of fellowship and made plans to move to Eufaula, Oklahoma, where another pastor friend had offered me some free space to open offices for the mission.

On the last day at the church, I tearfully preached my farewell sermon. When the last goodbye was said and the last hand was grasped, I locked the door and paused on the steps. I felt the hands of God lifting the mantle from my shoulders. God was releasing me of the burden for this church and the people of this place. As I strolled across the gravel driveway, the final mystery of Christian service became real to me.

Pastors — like missionary evangelists — are placed in the harvest fields of this world by God. No mission society, denomination, bishop, pope or superintendent calls a person to such service. In Gospel for Asia, I would not presume to ordain and call the native brethren, but simply be a servant to the ones whom God already had chosen for His service.

Seeking counsel from older Christian leaders, I eagerly listened to anyone who would give me advice. Everywhere I went I asked questions.

And I received offers of some strange help from various leaders. One dear man, a Christian executive who had spent a lifetime organizing another mission, just smiled in amusement when I asked for his advice.

"Here," he said, trying to be sensible and helpful, "the best advice I can give is this. Let me take over the support of the men you've committed yourself to in India. Give up this thing and just go back to India. People here will never trust you. In fact, it's impossible for them to do what you're suggesting."

That, of course, wasn't what I was ready to hear. I knew God had called me, and much of the advice I got was similarly suicidal and destructive. I found we had to learn most of our lessons by painful trial and error. The only way I escaped several disastrous decisions was my stubborn refusal to compromise the vision God had given. If something fit in with what God had said to me, then I considered it. If not — no matter how attractive it appeared — I refused. The secret of following God's will, I discovered, usually is wrapped up in rejecting the good for God's best.

One piece of advice did stick, however. Every Christian leader should have this engraved in his subconsciousness: *No matter what you do, never take yourself too seriously.* Paul Smith, founder of Bible Translations on Tape, was the first executive to say that to me, and I think it's one of the best single fragments of wisdom I've received from anyone.

God always chooses the foolish things of this world to confound the wise. He shows His might only on the behalf of those who trust in Him. *Humility is the place where all Christian service begins.*

7

Beginning to Feel
Like a Beggar

It didn't take long for me to make some early mistakes, and I couldn't afford any of them. We began the mission penniless, and I soon learned that even printing simple prayer letters and postage are a big expense.

We began without any kind of plan for regular involvement, but God soon gave us one. On one of my first trips, I went to Wheaton, Illinois. There I called on almost all the evangelical mission leaders. A few encouraged me — but not one offered the money we then needed desperately to keep going another day. The friend I stayed with, however, suggested we start a sponsorship plan through which North American families and individuals could support a native missionary regularly. It turned out to be just what we needed.

The idea — to lay aside one dollar a day for a native evangelist — gave us an instant handle for a program anyone could understand. I asked everyone I met if he or she would sponsor a native missionary for one dollar a day. Some said yes, and that's how the mission began to get regular donors.

Today, the "Dollar-a-Day" Pledge Plan is still the heart of our fund-raising efforts. We send the money — one hundred percent of it — to the field. Today we are sponsoring thousands of missionaries each month in this way.

Since I was sending all the pledge money overseas, we still

were faced with the need to cover our overhead and living expenses here in the United States. Time and time again — just when we were at our lowest point — God miraculously intervened to keep us and the ministry going.

One Sunday when we were down to our last dollar, I drove our old $125 Nova to a nearby church for worship. I knew no one and sat in the last row. When it came time to take the offering, I quickly made an excuse to God and held on to that last dollar.

"This is my last dollar," I prayed desperately, "and I need to buy gas just to get back home."

But knowing God loves a cheerful giver, I stopped fighting and sacrificed that last dollar to the Lord. The plate came by, and I dropped in the dollar.

As I left the church, an old man came up to me. I had never seen him before and never have since. He shook my hand silently, and I could feel a folded piece of paper in his palm. I knew instinctively that it was money. In the car, I opened my hand to find a neatly folded ten dollar bill.

Another afternoon, I sat grimly sulking on our sofa in Eufaula. Gisela was busy in the kitchen, avoiding my eyes. She said nothing, but both of us knew there wasn't any food in the house.

"So," said a coy voice from the enemy, "this is how you and your God provide for the family, eh?" Up until that moment, I don't think I'd ever felt such helplessness. Here we were, in the middle of Oklahoma. Even if I'd wanted to ask someone for help, I didn't know where to turn. Things had gotten so low I had offered to get a job, but Gisela was the one who refused. She was terrified that I would get into the world of business and not have time to work for the native brethren. For her there was no choice. It was wait on the Lord. He would provide.

As the demonic voice continued to taunt me, I just sat still under the abuse. I'd used up my last bit of faith, declaring a positive confession and praising God. Now I sat numb.

A knock came at the door.

Gisela went to answer it. I was in no mood to meet anyone.

Someone brought two boxes of groceries to our doorstep. These friends had no way of knowing our need—but we knew the source was God.

During those days our needs continued to be met on a day-to-day basis, and I never had to borrow from the missionary support funds. I am convinced now that God knew the many trials ahead and wanted to teach us to have faith and trust in Him alone—even when I couldn't see Him.

In some way, which I still don't really understand, the trying of our faith works patience and hope into the fabric of our Christian lives. No one, I am convinced, will follow Jesus very long without tribulation. It is His way of demonstrating His presence.

Sufferings and trials — like persecution — are a normal part of the Christian walk. We must learn to accept them joyfully if we are to grow through them, and I think this is true for ministries as well as individuals.

Gospel for Asia was having its first wilderness experience, and the Oklahoma days were characterized by periods of the most painful waiting I'd ever faced. We were alone in a strange land, utterly at the end of our own strength and desperately dependent on God.

Speaking engagements were hard to come by in the early days, but they were the only way we could grow. Nobody knew my name or the name of Gospel for Asia. I still was having a hard time explaining what we were all about. I knew our mission in my heart, but I hadn't learned to articulate it yet for outsiders. In a few short months, I had used up all the contacts I had.

Setting up a speaking tour took weeks of waiting, writing and calling. By the winter of 1980, however, I was ready to start on my first major tour. I bought a budget air ticket that gave me unlimited travel for twenty-one days — and somehow I managed to make appointments in eighteen cities. My itinerary would take me through the Southwest, from Dallas to Los Angeles.

On the day of my departure, a terrible winter storm hit the region. All the buses — including the one I planned to take from

Eufaula, Oklahoma, to Dallas — were cancelled.

We had an old 1969 Nova that had some engine problems, so a neighbor offered to let me use an old pick-up truck without a heater. The vehicle looked as if it couldn't make it to the next town, let alone the six-hour drive to Dallas. But it was either the pick-up or nothing.

If I missed my flight, the tightly packed schedule would be ruined. I just had to go now.

Doing the best I could to stay warm, I put on two pairs of socks and all the clothing I could. But even with the extra protection, I was on U.S. Highway 75 only a few minutes when it appeared I'd made a terrible mistake.

A freezing snow covered the windshield within minutes. Every mile I would have to stop, get out and scrape the windows again. After doing this one or two times, my feet and gloves were soaked and frozen. I realized that the journey, usually only four hours long, was going to take a lot longer than the six hours I had left. If I made it to Dallas, the trip would take twelve hours at this rate.

And the emphasis of that statement should be placed on the "if." In my worst scenario, I saw the newspaper headlines reading "Preacher Freezes to Death in Winter Storm." My head dropped to the steering wheel, and I cried out to God.

"Lord, if You want me to go — if You believe in this mission and in my helping the native evangelists — please do something."

As I looked up, I saw a miracle on the windshield. The ice was melting rapidly before my eyes. A warmth flooded the truck. I looked at the heater, but nothing was coming out. Some miraculous source of heat was filling the cab. Outside the storm continued to rage. It kept up all the way to Dallas, but the truck was always warm, and the windshield was always clear.

This miraculous start was only the beginning of blessings. For the next eighteen days, I gained new sponsors and donors in every city. The Lord gave me favor in the eyes of all I met.

On the last day of the tour, a man in California came up to the pastor and said God had told him to donate his second car to me.

I cancelled my airline reservation and drove all the way home, rejoicing in the car God had provided — and receiving new inspiration and instruction from God as I drove.

This is the pattern I was to follow for the next few years. I survived from one meeting to the next, living out of the trunk of the car and speaking anywhere I could get an invitation.

All our new donors and sponsors came from one-on-one contacts and through the meetings.

I knew there were faster, more efficient ways to acquire new donors. Many times I would look at the mass mailings and radio/TV broadcasts of other missions. But everything they were doing required large sums of money I didn't have and didn't know how to get.

Eventually, we moved back to Dallas. By now I was traveling full time for the ministry, and the strain was taking a heavy toll both on my family and on me. I was starting to burn out — and I almost hated the work.

Two factors were wearing me down.

First, I felt like a beggar. It is hard on the flesh to be traveling and asking for money day after day and night after night. It was almost becoming a sales operation for me, and I stopped feeling good about myself.

Second, I was discouraged by the poor response — especially from churches and pastors. Many times it seemed to me my presence threatened them. Where, I wondered, was the fraternal fellowship of working together in the extension of the kingdom? Many days I would call on people for hours to get only one or two new sponsors. Pastors and mission committees would listen to me and promise to call back, but I would never hear from them again.

It seemed as though I always was competing against the building fund, new carpets for the fellowship hall or next Saturday night's Jesus rock concert.

Despite the solemn message of death, suffering and need I was presenting, people still would leave the meetings with laughter and gossip on their lips. I was offended at the spirit of jocularity

71

in the churches. It wounded me. So many times we would go to eat after I had just shared the tragedy of the thousands who starve to death daily or the millions of homeless people living in the streets of Asia.

Because of this, I was becoming angry and judgmental. As I felt uglier and uglier inside, depression settled in.

Early in 1981 — while driving alone between meetings in a borrowed car near Greensboro, North Carolina — all the dark feelings of psychological burn-out crept over me. I was having a full-fledged pity party, feeling sorry for myself and the hard life I was leading.

With a start, I began to tremble with fear. Suddenly I felt the presence of someone else. I realized that the Spirit of the Lord was speaking.

"I am not in any trouble," He chided, "that I need someone to beg for Me or help Me out. I made no promises that I will not keep.

"It is not the largeness of the work that matters, but only doing what I command. All I ask of you is that you be a servant.

"For all who join with you in the work, it will be a privilege — a light burden for them."

The words echoed in my mind. This is His work, I told myself. Why am I making it mine? The burden is light. Why am I making it heavy? The work is a privilege. Why am I making it a chore?

I instantly repented of my sinful attitudes. God was sharing His work with me, and He was speaking of others who would join me. Although I still was doing the work alone, it was exciting to think others would be joining with me and that they too would find the burden to be light.

From that moment until this, I have not been overpowered by the burden of heading Gospel for Asia. I find building this mission an exciting, joyful job. Even my preaching has changed. My posture is different. Today the pressure is off. No more do I feel I have to beg audiences or make them feel guilty.

Since the work of Gospel for Asia — and the whole native missionary movement — is initiated by God, it doesn't need the worries and guidance of man.

Whether our goal is to support ten thousand or ten million missionaries, whether it is working in ten states or a hundred, or whether I must supervise a staff of five or five hundred, I still can approach this work without stress. For this is His work, and our burden is easy.

By now we had rented offices in Dallas, and the mission was growing steadily. I sensed it was time for a big step forward. I waited upon God for a miracle breakthrough. We had hundreds of native missionaries waiting for support by mid-1981, and I realized that we soon would have thousands more. I no longer could communicate personally with every new sponsor. I knew we had to use mass media.

But I didn't know where to begin.

Then it happened. I met Brother Lester Roloff.

Roloff now is with the Lord, but during his life he was a rugged individualist who preached his way across five decades of outstanding Christian service.

Near the end of his life, I approached him for help in our ministry. His staff person, in arranging the interview, said I would have only five minutes. They were astonished when he gave me two hours of his time.

When I told him about the native missionary movement, he invited me to be his guest on the "Family Altar" — his daily radio broadcast. At that time we were helping only one hundred native missionaries, and Roloff announced over the air that he personally was going to sponsor six more. He called me one of the "greatest missionaries he had ever met" and urged his listeners to sponsor native missionaries as well. Soon we were getting letters from all over the country.

As I read the postmarks and the letters, I realized again how huge the United States and Canada are. Roloff was the first Christian leader I'd ever met who already had done what I knew we needed to do. He'd learned how to speak to the whole nation.

For weeks I prayed for him, asking God to show me how I

could work with him and learn from his example.

When the answer came, it was quite different from anything I had expected. The Lord gave me an idea which I now realize was unusual, almost bizarre. I would ask Roloff to loan me his mailing list and let me ask his people to sponsor a native missionary.

Trembling, I called his office and asked for another appointment. He saw me again but was very surprised at my request.

He told me that he'd never done anything like that before and had never loaned his list to anyone — even his best friends. Many agencies had asked to rent his list, but he had always said no. I thought my cause was lost, but he said he would pray about it.

The next day he called me back. He said the Lord had told him to give us his list. He also offered to write a letter of endorsement and interview me again on the radio broadcast at the same time the letter went out.

Elated, I praised God. But I soon learned that this was only the beginning of the miracle.

The list was a fairly large one, and to print a brochure, my letter and his letter, together with the mailing, would cost more money than we had.

There seemed to be only one way to get it. I would have to borrow — just once — from the missionary funds. I figured it out again and again. If I worked it just right, I could get the money to the field with only a few weeks' delay. But I had no peace about the plan. I'd always used the funds exactly as designated.

It came time to send the regular monies to the field. I told our bookkeeper to hold the money for one day, and I prayed. Still no peace. The next day I told her to hold the money up for another day, and I went back to prayer and fasting. Still no peace. I delayed it for a third day — and still God wouldn't release me to use the missionary support funds.

I was miserable. Finally I decided that I couldn't break the trust of our donors — even for the Lord's work. I told my secretary to go ahead and send the missionary money.

I now realize we had gone through one of the greatest tests of the ministry. This was it, my first chance to get a major increase in donors and income — but it had to be done with integrity, or not at all.

A half hour after the check had gone off to the field, the phone rang. It was from a couple whom I had met only once before at our annual banquet in Dallas.

They had been praying about helping us, and God had laid me on their hearts. They asked if they could come and talk to me, and they wanted to know what I needed.

After I explained the cost involved for printing and putting out the mailing, they agreed to pick up the entire amount of this project, which was nearly twenty thousand dollars. Then the printer became so moved by the project that he did it for free! Plainly God had been testing me, and He miraculously showed that if we were obedient, He indeed would provide.

The art work went off to the printers and soon printed letters were sitting on skids, ready for the post office. I had prepared a special radio broadcast to coincide with the arrival of the mailing — and the broadcast tapes already had been shipped to the stations in many parts of the nation.

Timing was everything. The mail had to go on Monday. It was Friday, and I didn't have undesignated money in the general fund for the postage. This time there was no question of borrowing the missionary money. It stayed right where it was.

I called a special prayer meeting, and we met that night in the living room of our home. Finally the Lord gave me peace. Our prayers of faith would be answered, I announced. After everyone had gone home, the phone rang.

It was one of our sponsors in Chicago. God had been speaking to her all day about giving a five thousand dollar gift.

"Praise God," I said.

That mailing incident proved to be another turning point in the history of Gospel for Asia. We received many new sponsors — a double increase in the number of evangelists we were able to sponsor.

In later years, other Christian leaders like Bob Walker of Christian Life Missions and David Mains of "Chapel of the Air" would help us in similar ways. Many of the people who joined our ministry through those several early mailings have since helped to expand the ministry even further, giving us a base of contacts from every state in the union.

God had given us a clear message for the body of Christ — *a call to recover the church's missionary mandate.*

In every place, I preached this same message — a prophetic cry to my brothers and sisters in Christ on behalf of the lost millions in the Third World. Through it, thousands of believers started to change their life-styles and conform to the demands of the gospel.

8

Missions Are Not Dead; the Leadership Is Changing Hands

Several hundred dedicated believers now were supporting native missionaries. But despite this aura of success, many things broke my heart, especially the condition of American Christians. What had happened to the zeal for missions and outreach that made this nation so great? Night after night I would stand before audiences, trying the best I could to communicate the global realities of our planet. But somehow I wasn't getting through. *I could see their unfulfilled destiny so clearly. Why couldn't they?*

Here were people of great privilege — a nation which is more able, more affluent and more free to act on the Great Commission than any other in all history. Yet my audiences didn't seem to comprehend this. Even more confusing to me was the fact that in personal dealings I found my hosts to be basically fair, often generous, and spiritually gifted. Like the church in first-century Corinth, it appeared to excel in every spiritual blessing.

Why then, I asked the Lord, wasn't I getting through?

If the native missionary movement was really the will of God — and I knew it was — then why were the people so slow to respond?

Something obviously had gone very wrong. Satan had sprung a trap, or perhaps many traps, on the minds of Western Christians. It was plain to see they had lost the gospel mandate. They had abdicated the heritage of missionary outreach, the call of God that still rests on this nation.

In my prayers I began to seek a message from God that would bring a change in life-style to the church. It came over a period of weeks. And that message came loud and clear: *Unless there is repentance among Christians—individually and in concert as a community of believers—an awesome judgment will fall on America.*

I was certain then, and still am today, that God's loving hands of grace and forgiveness remain extended to His people. Two reasons, it appeared to me, were the cause for the current malaise that has fastened like cancer on American believers. The first is historical. The second is the unconfessed sins related to three basic iniquities: pride, unbelief and worldliness.

Historically, the Western church lost its grip on the challenge for world missions at the end of World War II — and ever since that time its moral mandate and vision for global outreach have continued to fade. Today the average North American believer can hardly pronounce the word "missionary" without having cartoon caricatures of ridiculous little men in pith helmets pop into mind — images of cannibals with spears and huge black pots of boiling water.

Despite a valiant rearguard action by many outstanding evangelical leaders and missions, it has been impossible for the Western missionary movement to keep up with exploding populations and the new political realities of nationalism in the Third World.

Most Christians in North America still conceive of missions in terms of blond-haired, blue-eyed white people going to the dark-skinned Third World nations. In reality, all of that changed at the end of World War II when the Western powers lost political and military control of their former colonies.

When I stand before North American audiences in churches and missions conferences, people are astonished to hear the real facts of missions today. The frontline work of missions in Asia has been taken over almost completely by indigenous missionaries. And the results are outstanding. Believers are shocked to learn that native missionaries are starting hundreds of new churches every week in the Third World, that thousands of people a day are being converted to Christ, and that tens of thousands of well-qualified, spiritually able men and women now are ready to start more mission work if we can raise their support.

In India, which no longer permits Western missionary evangelists, more church growth and outreach are happening now than at any point in our history.

China is another good example of the new realities. When the communists drove Western missionaries out and closed the churches in 1950, it seemed that Christianity was dead. In fact, most of the known leaders were imprisoned, and a whole generation of Chinese pastors was killed off or disappeared in communist prisons and torture chambers.

But today communication is open again with China, and we find forty thousand to fifty thousand underground churches have sprung up during the communist persecution. The number of Christians now has grown to an estimated fifty million — fifty times the size of the church when Western missionaries were driven out. All this again has happened under the spiritual direction of the indigenous church movement.

From a historical perspective, it is not difficult to trace how Western thinking has been confused by the march of history. In the early 1950s, the destruction of the colonial missionary establishment was big news. As the doors of China, India, Burma, North Korea, North Vietnam and many other newly independent nations slammed shut on Western missionaries, it was natural for the traditional churches and denominational missions to assume that their day had ended.

That, of course, was in itself untrue, as evidenced by the growth of evangelical missions in the same period. But many became convinced then that the age of missions had ended forever.

Except for the annual missions appeal in most churches, many North American believers lost hope of seeing the Great Commission of Christ fulfilled on a global scale. Although it was rarely stated, the implication was this: If North American or Western European-based mission boards aren't leading the way, then it can't happen.

Mission monies once used to proclaim the gospel were more and more sidetracked into the charitable social programs toward which the new governments of the former colonies were more sympathetic. A convenient theology of mission developed that today sometimes equates social and political action with evangelism.

Many of the Western missionaries who did stay on in Asia also were deeply affected by the rise of nationalism. They began a steady retreat from evangelism and discipleship, concentrating for the most part on broadcasting, education, medical, publishing, relief and social work. Missionaries, when home in the West, continued to give the impression that indigenization meant not only the pull-out of Western personnel but also the pull-out of financial and other assistance.

The debate among Western leaders about the future of missions has in the meantime raged on, producing whole libraries of books and some valuable research. Regrettably, however, the overall result on the average Christian has been extremely negative. Believers today have no idea that a new day in missions has dawned or that their support of missions is more desperately needed than ever before.

True, in many cases, it no longer is possible, for political reasons, for Western missionaries to go overseas, but American believers still have a vital role in helping us in the Third World finish the task. I praise God for the pioneer work done by Hudson Taylor and others like him who were sent by believers at home in the past. Now, in countries like India, we need instead to send financial and technical support to native evangelists and Bible teachers.

Imagine the implications of being involved in the work of the Great Commission, of getting your church and family to join with you in supporting native missions.

Picture this very possible scene. You finish your life on this earth. You arrive in heaven. There, enthroned in all His glory, is our Lord Jesus Christ. The other saints and martyrs you've so often read about are there: Abraham, Moses, Peter and Paul, plus great leaders from more recent times. Your family and loved ones who obeyed the gospel also are there. They are all welcoming you into heaven.

You walk around in bliss, filled with joy and praises. All the promises of the Bible are true. The streets really are gold, and the glory of God shines brightly, replacing the sun, moon and stars. It is beyond the power of any man to describe.

Then, scores of strangers whom you don't recognize start to gather around with happy smiles and outstretched hands. They embrace you with affection and gratitude.

"Thank you....Thank you....Thank you," they repeat in a chorus. With great surprise you ask, "What did I do? I have never seen you before."

Then they tell you the story of how they came to be in heaven, all because your love and concern reached out to them while they were on earth. You see that these persons come from "every tongue and tribe," just as the Bible says — from India, Bangladesh, Bhutan, Thailand and the Philippines.

"But what exactly did I do?" you ask. Then, like a replay of a videotape, your mind goes back to a day of your life on earth when a local mission coordinator came to your church. He told you about the lost millions of Asia — about the 300 million who have never heard the gospel in India alone. He told you about the desperately poor native missionaries and challenged you to support them.

You were one of those who said yes. The crowd of Asians continue: "As a result of your support, one of our own — a native evangelist — came to us and preached the gospel of the kingdom. He lived simply like us, speaking our language and dressed in our clothing. We were able to accept his message easily.

"We were serving idols and never had the opportunity to hear the gospel until he came and preached to us. We learned for the first time about the love of Jesus, who died on the cross for us, and how His blood redeemed us from sin, Satan and death."

As the crowd finishes, several whole families come up to you. You can see the tenderness and gratefulness on their faces as well. They join the others, taking you in their arms and thanking you again.

"How can we ever express our appreciation for the love and kindness you showed to us on the earth? We were struggling in the service of the Lord. Often we went without food. Our children cried for milk, but we had none to give. Unknown and forsaken by our own people, we sought to witness to our own people who had never heard the gospel. Now they are here in eternity with us.

"In the middle of our suffering, you came into our lives with your prayers and financial support. Your help relieved us so much — making it possible for us to carry on the work of the Lord. We are one of the missionary families you supported in Asia.

"We never had a chance to see you face-to-face in the world. Now we can see you here and spend all eternity rejoicing with you over the victories of the Lord."

Now Jesus Himself appears. You bow as He quotes the familiar Scripture verses to you: "I was an hungered, and ye gave me meat: I was thirsty, and ye gave me drink: I was a stranger, and ye took me in: naked, and ye clothed Me....Verily I say unto you, Inasmuch as ye have done it unto one of the least of these my brethren, ye have done it unto me" (Matt. 25:35-40).

Is this just a fanciful story, or will it be reality for many thousands of North American Christians? I believe it could happen as Christians arrive in heaven and see how they have laid up treasure where moth and rust cannot corrupt.

Every time I stand before an audience, I try to ask two very important questions early in my message:

• Why do you think God has allowed you to be born in North America or Western Europe and to be blessed with such material and spiritual abundance?

• In light of the super-abundance you enjoy here, what do you think is your minimal responsibility to the untold millions of lost and suffering in the Third World?

Every Christian needs to ask himself why God allowed him or her to be born here rather than among the poor masses of Africa and Asia. Did you earn that right?

What does it mean to be born among the privileged elite of this world? Why do you have so much when others have so little? Think a moment about the vast difference between your country and the nations without a Christian heritage.

The material abundance here is staggering. One-fourth of the world lives on an income of less than three dollars a week — most of them in Asia. The gross national product per person in South Asia is only $180 a year. Americans earn an average of fifty-four times more — and Christian Americans, because they tend to live in the upper half of the economy, earn even more.[1]

In most countries where Gospel for Asia is serving the native missionary movement, a good wage is one dollar to three dollars a day. While much of the world is concerned mainly about where its next meal is coming from, affluent North Americans spend most of their wages and waking moments planning unnecessary purchases.

In the United States, Canada and Western Europe, there is freedom of choice. Political freedoms of speech, press and assembly are just part of the picture. There is freedom to worship and organize religious ministries and to choose where and how to live. Citizens are free to organize themselves to correct injustices and problems both at home and abroad.

Moreover, there is leisure time and disposable income. Although these are not written into law, citizens are free from the basic wants that make living so difficult in many other parts of the world.

Also, a large number of service networks are available which make it easy to effect change, such as communications, education, finance, mass media and transportation. Not having these services available is an enormous handicap to people in most other parts of the world.

Finally, few domestic needs exist. While unemployment is a serious problem in some areas, it is many times higher in nearly every country of the Third World. How many of us can comprehend the suffering of the millions of homeless and starving people in nations like Bangladesh? Overseas the problems are on a grand scale. Some nations struggle to help themselves but still fail woefully.

This list is just illustrative of the many advantages of living in the Western world where benefits have come *largely because of a Christian heritage.*

Part II

THE CALL

9

You Have Destroyed Everything
We Were Trying to Do

If the apostle Paul had not brought the gospel to Europe, the foundation principles of freedom and human dignity would not be part of the American heritage. Because the Holy Spirit instructed him to turn away from Asia and go west, America has been blessed with its systems of law and economics — the principles that made it rich and free.

In addition, America is the only nation in the world founded by believers in Christ who made a covenant with God — dedicating a new nation to God.

Born into affluence, freedom and divine blessings, Americans should be the most thankful people on earth. But along with the privilege comes a responsibility.

The Christian must ask not only why but what should he or she do with these unearned favors?

Throughout Scripture, there is only one correct response to abundance: *sharing*.

God gives some people more than they need so that they can be channels of blessing to others. God desires equity between His people on a worldwide basis. That is why the early church had no poverty.

"Our desire," wrote the apostle Paul to the rich Christians in Corinth, "is not that others might be relieved while you are hard pressed, but that there might be equality. At the present time your plenty will supply what they need, so that in turn their plenty will supply what you need. Then there will be equality" (2 Cor. 8:13,14, NIV).

The Bible advocates and demands that we show love for the needy brethren. Right now, because of historical and economic factors that none of us can control, the needy brethren are in Asia. The wealthy brethren are in the United States, Canada and a few other nations. The conclusion is obvious: These affluent believers must share with the poorer churches.

"We know we have passed from death to life, because we love our brothers....If anyone has material possessions and sees his brother in need but has no pity on him, how can the love of God be in him? Dear children, let us not love with words or tongue but with actions and in truth" (1 John 3:14-18, NIV).

And, "What doth it profit, my brethren, though a man say he hath faith, and have not works? can faith save him? If a brother or sister be naked and destitute of daily food, and one of you say unto them, Depart in peace, be ye warmed and filled; notwithstanding ye give them not those things which are needful to the body; what doth it profit? Even so faith, if it hath not works, is dead, being alone" (James 2:14-17).

Is missions an option — especially for super-wealthy countries like America? The biblical answer is clear. Every Christian in America has some minimal responsibility to get involved in helping the poor brethren in the church in other countries.

God has not given this superabundance of blessings to American and Canadian Christians so that we only can sit back and enjoy the luxuries of this society — or even in spiritual terms, so that we can gorge ourselves on books, teaching cassettes and deeper-life conferences. He has left us on this earth to be stewards of these spiritual and material blessings. God wants us to become experts on how to share with others.

Believers have a date with destiny. They are to be servants to the expanding churches and movements of God around the world. We need to gain a sense of trusteeship, learning to administer our wealth to accomplish the purposes of God.

What then is the bottom line? God is calling us as Christians to alter our life-styles. We must find ways to give up the non-essentials of our lives so that we can better invest our wealth in the kingdom of God.

To start, I challenge believers to lay aside at least one dollar a day to support a native missionary in the Third World. This, of course, should be over and above our present commitments to the local church and other ministries.

I do not ask Christians to redirect their giving away from other ministries for native missions — but to expand their giving over and above current levels. Most people can do this.

For many North American and Western European believers — millions of them — this can be accomplished easily simply by giving up cookies, cakes, sweets, coffee and other beverages. Many of these junk foods harm our bodies anyway, and anyone can save enough in this way to sponsor one or even two missionaries a month.

Many are going beyond this and, without affecting health or happiness, are able to sponsor several missionaries every month.

Of course, there are many other ways to get involved. Some cannot give more financially, but they can invest time in prayer and serve as volunteer coordinators to help recruit more sponsors. And a few are called to go overseas to become involved experientially.

The single most important hindrance to world evangelization right now is the lack of total involvement by the body of Christ. I am convinced there are enough potential sponsors to support all the native missionaries needed to evangelize the Third World.

It's true the native missionary movement is relatively new, and many Christians still haven't been challenged to participate, but that is superficial. The real truth is much more basic — and more deadly.

Ask the average person why the Lord destroyed Sodom, and he will cite the city's gross immorality. However, Ezekiel reveals the real reason in chapter 16, verses 49 and 50: "Behold this was the guilt of your sister Sodom: she and her daughters had pride, surfeit of food, and prosperous ease, but did not aid the poor and needy. They were haughty and did abominable things before me; therefore I removed them, when I saw it."

Sodom refused to aid the needy poor because of pride. We are caught up in a national pride similar to Sodom's. Admittedly, from that pride also come selfishness and perversion, but we need to see that pride is the real root. Deal with that root and you cut off a multitude of sins before they have a chance to grow. One night while speaking at a church missionary conference, I was asked to meet privately with the church council to give my reaction to a new mission program they were considering. This was in a grand old church with a large mission budget.

I already had preached and was very tired. I didn't really want to sit in on a board meeting. By the time everyone arrived, there were twenty-two in the room. The meeting began in the usual way, more like a corporate board meeting at IBM or General Motors than a church board.

The presenter made an impressive, business-like proposal. The scheme involved shifting "third country nationals" from Asia to a mission field in Latin America. It was very futuristic and sounded like a major leap in missions, but warning lights and bells were going off in my mind. To me it sounded like nineteenth-century colonial missionary practice dressed up in a different disguise.

The Lord spoke to me clearly: "Son, tonight you must speak to people who are so self-sufficient they've never asked Me about this plan. They think I'm helpless."

So when the chairman of the church council finally called on me to respond with my opinion of the proposal, I stood and read certain parts of Matthew 28:18-20:

"All power is given unto Me in heaven and in earth. Go ye therefore and teach all nations...to observe all things that I have commanded you: and, lo, I am with you always...."

Then I closed my Bible and paused, looking each one in the eye.

"If He is with you," I said, "then you will represent Him —

not just be like Him — but you will exercise His authority. Where is the power of God in this plan?"

I didn't need to say much. The Holy Spirit anointed my words, and everyone seemed to understand.

"How often have you met for prayer?" I asked rhetorically. "How long since you have had an entire day of prayer to seek God's mind about your mission strategy?" From their eyes it was easy to see they had prayed little about their mission budget, which was then in the hundreds of thousands of dollars.

So little of evangelical Christian work is done in total dependence upon the living God. We have devised methods, plans and techniques to "do" God's work. Those involved apparently do not sense a need to pray or be filled with the Holy Spirit to do the work of Jesus.

How far we have drifted from the faith of the apostles and the prophets. What a tragedy that the techniques of the world and its agents are brought into the sanctuary of God.

Only when we are emptied of our own self-sufficiency can God use us. When a church or a mission board spends more time in consultation, planning and committee meetings than in prayer, it is a clear indication the members have lost touch with the supernatural and have ended up, in Watchman Nee's words, "serving the house of God and forgot the Lord Himself."

The discussion went on until 1:30 in the morning, but with a new sense of repentance in the room.

"Brother K.P.," said the leader to me afterwards, "you have destroyed everything we were trying to do tonight, but now we're ready to wait on God for His plan." This is the kind of humility that will bring the church back into the center of God's will and global plan. Churches today are not experiencing the power and anointing of God in their ministries because they don't have the humility to wait on Him, and because of that sin, the world remains largely unreached.

Part of this pride is a subtle but very deep racism. In many of my meetings, I will hear innocent-sounding questions such as, How do we know that the native church is ready to handle the funds? or, What kind of training have the native missionaries had?

So long as such questions are based on a sincere desire for good stewardship, they are commendable. But in many cases, I have found the intent of the question is something much less honorable.

Westerners refuse to trust Asians the way they trust their own people. If we're satisfied that a certain native missionary is truly called to the gospel, we have to trust God and turn our stewardship over to him and his elders just as we would to another brother in our own culture. To expect to continue controlling the use of money and the ministry overseas from our foreign-based mission board is an extension of colonialism. It adds an unbiblical element which only humiliates and weakens the native missionary in the long run.

What Christians need to learn is that they're not giving *their money* to native workers, but *God's money* to His work overseas.

Churches need to develop the quiet disciplines they have lost — practices such as contemplation, fasting, listening, meditation, prayer, silence, Scripture memory, submission and reflection.

Instead of glorifying two-fisted fighters in the John Wayne tradition of American folk heroes, Christians would do well to sit still until the power of God is manifested in their Christian activities.

Many Christian leaders are caught up in secondary issues that sap their time and energy.

I'll never forget preaching in one church where the pastor had turned defending the King James translation of the Bible into a crusade. Not only does he spend most of his pulpit time upholding it — but thousands of dollars go to printing books, tracts and pamphlets advocating the exclusive use of this one translation.

In the years I have lived and worked in the United States, I have watched believers and whole congregations get caught up in all kinds of similar crusades and causes which, while not necessarily bad in themselves, end up taking our eyes off obedience to Christ. And in this sense, they become anti-Christ.

Red-hot issues that burn across the horizon — like inerrancy, versions of the Bible, charismatic gifts, the latest revelations of itinerant teachers, secular humanism, or whatever new issue raises its head tomorrow — need to be kept in their proper perspective. There always will be new dragons to slay, but we must not let these side battles keep us from our main task of building and expanding the kingdom of God.

When I go to Asia, I see our churches and theologians there being just as violently divided over a different set of issues, and through this I have come to realize that many times these doctrinal divisions are being used by the evil one to keep us preoccupied with something other than the gospel.

We are driven by powerful egos always to be right. We are often slaves to a strong tendency to "have it our way." All these are manifestations of pride. The opposite of that is the servanthood commanded by Christ.

Making a sacrifice for one of the unknown brethren — supporting his work to a strange people in a strange place, using methods that are a mystery to you — does take humility.

But supporting the native brethren must begin with this kind of commitment to humility and must continue in the same spirit. Sadly, our pride all too often stands in the way of progress.

10

God Is Withholding Judgment

Early in my ministry I learned to beware of boasters. They're usually covering up something. One of the great boasts of many Western born-again, evangelical Christians is their devotion to Scripture. It's hard to find a Christian organization that doesn't at one time or another brag about being "Bible believing." When I first came here, I made the mistake of taking that description at face value.

In reality, I have come to see that many evangelical Christians don't really believe the Word of God. Instead they selectively accept only the portions that allow them to continue living in their current life-styles.

I'm talking about hell and judgment. These are lost teachings. Believers are willing to accept the concept of heaven, but they look the other way when they come to passages about hell. Very few seem to believe that those who die without Christ are going to a place where they are tormented forever and ever in a bottomless pit where the fire is not quenched; where they are separated from God and His love for all eternity without any chance of return.

Why aren't Christians living in obedience to God? Because of their unbelief.

Why did Eve fall into sin? Because she didn't truly believe in the judgment — that death really would come if she ate what God forbade. This is the same reason many continue in their lives of sin and disobedience.

It's painful to think about hell and judgment. I understand why preachers don't like to talk about it, because I don't either. It's so much easier to preach that "God loves you and has a wonderful plan for your life" or to focus on the many delightful aspects of possibility thinking and the word of faith that brings health, wealth and happiness. The grace and love of God are pleasant subjects, and no one more beautifully demonstrated them than our Lord Jesus. Yet in His earthly ministry, He made more references to hell and judgment than He did to heaven.

Jesus lived with the reality of hell, and He died on Calvary because He knew it was real and coming to everyone who doesn't turn to God in this life.

If we knew the horrors of the potential judgment that hangs over us — if we really believed in what's coming — how differently we would live. The Great Depression and current recessions are only a slap on the wrist compared to the poverty that lies ahead — let alone the bombs, disease and natural calamities. But God is withholding judgment now to give us time to repent.

Unfortunately, for millions in the Third World, it will be too late unless we can reach them before they slip off the edge into eternal darkness.

For years I have struggled with making this a reality in our meetings. Finally I found a way.

I ask my listeners to hold their wrists and find their pulse. Then I explain that every beat they feel represents the death of someone in Asia who had died and gone to eternal hell without ever hearing the good news of Jesus Christ even once.

"What if one of those beats represented your own mother?" I ask. "Your own father, your spouse, your child...you yourself?"

These millions of Asians who are dying and going to hell are people for whom Christ died. We say we believe it — but what are we doing to act on that faith? Without works, faith is dead.

There's no reason why anyone should go to hell today without hearing about the Lord Jesus. To me this is an atrocity much worse than the death camps of Hitler's Germany or Stalin's Russia. As horrible as the 1.5 million annual abortions are in the United States each year, the eternal loss of multiplied millions of additional souls every year is the greatest preventable tragedy of our times.

If only a small percentage of the fifty million people who claim to be born-again Christians in this country were to sponsor a native missionary, we could have literally hundreds of thousands of evangelists reaching the lost villages of Asia.

When we look at the unfinished Great Commission and compare it to our personal life-styles — or to the activity calendars of our churches and organizations — how can we explain our disobedience? There is only one conclusion — we must see a great repentance from the sin of unbelief.

C.T. Studd, the famous British athlete and founder of Worldwide Evangelization Crusade, was one who gave up all his achievements in this life for Christ's sake. He was challenged to his commitment by an article written by an atheist. That article in part said:

> If I firmly believed, as millions say they do, that the knowledge and practice of religion in this life influences destiny in another, then religion would mean to me everything.
>
> I would cast away earthly enjoyments as dross, earthly cares as follies, and earthly thoughts and feelings as vanity. Religion would be my first waking thought and my last image before sleep sank me into unconsciousness. I should labor in its cause alone.
>
> I would take thought for the morrow of eternity alone. I would esteem one soul gained for heaven worth a life of suffering.
>
> Earthly consequences would never stay my hand, or seal my lips. Earth, its joys and its griefs, would occupy no moment of my thoughts. I would

strive to look upon eternity alone, and on the immortal souls around me, soon to be everlastingly happy
or everlastingly miserable.

I would go forth to the world and preach to it in
season and out of season, and my text would be:

"For what is a man profited, if he shall gain the
whole world, and lose his own soul?"[1]

Another iniquity plaguing the Western church is worldliness.
Once, on a two-thousand-mile auto trip across the American
West, I made it a point to listen to Christian radio all along the
way. What I heard revealed much about the secret motivations
that drive many Christians. Some of the broadcasts would have
been hilarious if they weren't exploiting the gullible — hawking
health, wealth and success in the name of Christianity.

• Holy oil and lucky charms were offered to those who sent
in money and requested them. Instant material blessings were
promised.

• Prayer cloths were offered which had blessed believers with
$70,000 — $100,000 — new cars — houses — and health.

• Holy soap would be mailed to others who requested it. It
had been blessed by the speaker. If used with his instructions, it
would wash away bad luck, evil friends and sickness. Again he
promised "plenty of money" and everything else the user wanted.

While such con games bring a smile to our lips, the same basic
package is marketed with more sophistication at every level of
this society. Christian magazines, TV shows and church services
often put the spotlight on famous athletes, beauty queens, businessmen and politicians who "make it in the world and have Jesus
too!"

Affinity group evangelism that targets Christians in athletics,
business, politics and media grabs headlines in the Christian
press — but where are the stories of those who target welfare
mothers, the sick, the divorced and inner-city poor who are dying
without Christ?

Today Christian values are defined almost totally by success as it is promoted by Madison Avenue advertising. Even many Christian ministries gauge their effectiveness by the standards of Harvard MBAs.

Jesus said the heart is where the treasures are kept. So what can we say about many evangelical Christians? Getting into debt for cars, homes and furnishings which probably are not needed; sacrificing family, church and health for corporate promotions and career advancement — I believe all this is deception, engineered by the god of this world to ensnare and destroy effective Christians.

"Love not the world," says John in his first epistle, "neither the things that are in the world. If any man love the world, the love of the Father is not in him. For all that is in the world, the lust of the flesh, and the lust of the eyes, and the pride of life, is not of the Father, but is of the world. And the world passeth away, and the lust thereof: but he that doeth the will of God abideth forever" (2:15-17).

The typical media testimony goes something like this: "I was sick and broke, a total failure. Then I met Jesus. Now everything is fine; my business is booming and I am a great success."

It sounds wonderful. Be a Christian and get that bigger house and a boat and vacation in the Holy Land.

But if that were really God's way, it would put some Christians behind the Iron Curtain and in the Third World in a pretty bad light. Their testimonies often go something like this:

"I was happy. I had everything — prestige, recognition, a good job, and a happy wife and children. Then I gave my life to Jesus Christ. Now I am in Siberia, having lost my family, wealth, reputation, job and health.

"Here I live, lonely, deserted by friends. I cannot see the face of my wife and dear children. My crime is that I love Jesus."

What about the heroes of the faith down through the ages? Most of the apostles were martyred. John died in exile. Christian martyrs have written their names on every page of history.

In Russia, Ivan Moiseyev was tortured and killed within two years of meeting Jesus. In China, Watchman Nee spent twenty years in prison and finally died in bondage.

When Sadhu Sundar Singh, born and raised in a rich Sikh's home in the Punjab, became a Christian, his own family tried to poison him and banished him from their home. He lost his inheritance and walked away with one piece of cloth on his body. Yet, following his Master, he made millions truly rich through faith in Christ.

Our native missionaries supported by Gospel for Asia also often suffer for their commitment. Coming from Hindu and Muslim backgrounds, they often are literally thrown out of their homes, lose their jobs and are beaten and chased from their villages when they accept Christ.

They faithfully serve Christ daily, suffering untold hardship because Jesus promised His followers, "In this world ye shall have tribulation, but be of good cheer, I have overcome the world" (John 16:33).

What He promised were trials and tribulations. But we can face them because we know He already has won the battle. God does promise to meet our physical needs. And He does, indeed, bless His children materially. But He blesses us for a purpose — not so we can squander those resources on ourselves, but so we can be good stewards, using our resources wisely to win the lost to God's saving grace.

That is why Gisela and I have maintained a simple life-style over these years. We have not sought to accumulate wealth, but to be good stewards of that which God has given us. Our goal, of course, is to send all we can to help support the work of Asia's native missionaries.

The Scripture tells us, "Whoso hath this world's goods, and seeth his brother have need, and shutteth up his bowels of compassion from him, how dwelleth the love of God in him?" (1 John 3:17).

As A.W. Tozer, noted Christian and Missionary Alliance pastor and author, once said, "There is no doubt that the possessive clinging to things is one of the most harmful habits in life. Because it is so natural, it is rarely recognized for the evil that it is. But its outworkings are tragic. This ancient curse will not go out painlessly. The tough old miser within us will not lie down and die obedient to our command. He must be torn out, torn out of our hearts like a plant from the soil; he must be extracted in blood and agony like a tooth from the jaw. He must be expelled from our souls in violence as Christ expelled the money changers from the temple."

Let's face it, many Western believers are the rich young rulers of our day. Jesus is saying to them, "If thou wilt be perfect, go and sell all that thou hast, and give to the poor, and thou shalt have treasure in heaven: and come and follow me" (Matt. 19:16-24).

11

Why Should I Make Waves?

By the end of 1981 we appeared to be getting a measure of acceptance. People from all over the United States and Canada began to share with us in the ministry of equipping native missionaries to evangelize in their own countries.

But I wasn't satisfied. For some reason I became obsessed, almost neurotic, with a desire to gain greater respect and recognition for our ministry.

We joined the Evangelical Council for Financial Accountability and other associations, but nothing seemed to satisfy me. I didn't realize how insatiable my desire for recognition had become until one night in a little church in Victoria, Texas.

As Gisela and our office staff in Dallas worked to assign our new sponsors to native missionaries, I felt led of the Lord to plan a road tour of fourteen Texas towns to meet personally with new supporters. Calling ahead, I introduced myself and thanked the people for taking on the sponsorship of a native missionary.

I was stunned by the response. Most of the people had heard me on the radio and appeared thrilled with the idea of meeting me. In every town, someone invited me to stay with his family and made arrangements for me to speak in small house meetings and churches. People were referring to me in a new way — as the president and director of an important missionary organization. Far from being pleased, I was more terrified than ever — afraid that I would fail or be rejected.

Tour plans were completed. The meetings were booked solid, and publicity had gone out, but an unreasonable fear took over. A weariness settled upon me. As the day for my departure came closer, I looked for excuses to cancel or postpone going to meet the people and their pastors.

"My family and the office need me more," I argued. "Besides, I'll be driving alone. It's dangerous and difficult — I should really wait until someone can go with me."

Just when I had almost talked myself out of going, the Lord spoke to me in an unmistakable voice during my personal morning devotion. As on other occasions, it was just as if He were in the room with me. He spoke to me from John 10.

"My sheep hear My voice," said the Lord. "I know My own and My own know Me. My sheep follow Me because they know My voice." I didn't need an interpretation; the message was clear.

The trip, I realized, had been ordained by Him. He had arranged it and opened the doors for me. My response was to picture myself as a little lamb and follow my Shepherd over the highways and roads. He would go ahead of me to every church and every home in which I was to stay, I assured myself.

The Lord further confirmed my calling and renewed my courage as I prayed. He reminded me I was not speaking on behalf of K.P. Yohannan or Gospel for Asia.

"You will go where I send you," He said, "because you are representing My servants — the unknown brethren — and I am going with you." All I had to do was obey. I did, and it turned out to be a heavenly two weeks. In every home and church I had delightful fellowship with our new friends — and we added a number of additional supporters as a result of those meetings.

The church in Victoria, Texas, was almost my last stop and the Lord had a special surprise waiting for me there. But He had to prepare me first.

As I drove from town to town, I had time alone in the car for the Lord to deal with me on several issues that would have a lot to do with the future of the mission and my own walk with Him.

I had just read a book which told the story of one saint who had prayed for God to "stamp a vision of eternity in both his eyes." I couldn't shake the words of that strange prayer from my mind, and I soon found that I, too, was praying for the same kind of eternal perspective on life.

It was at this time I faced up to one of the most far-reaching policy decisions I ever would make. For some years I had suffered deep pain over the obvious impotence and waste of mission hospitals and schools in India. Now in America I was seeing new forms of the same thing — so many fine churches and Christians seemed to be preoccupied with the things of this world.

There appeared to be massive imbalance between our preoccupation with Christian institutions and the proclamation of the gospel. Both in India and in my travels around Western countries, I constantly uncovered a preoccupation with worldly activities operated by Christian organizations under the guise of "Christian ministry." Often there was little that was distinctively Christian about them — except, of course, that Christian workers operated them or church monies financed them.

One study, for instance, disclosed that nearly 80 percent of all North American missionaries overseas are involved primarily in social work. In contrast, less than a quarter of the American mission force overseas is left to work in evangelism and church planting. Peter Wagner, in his book *On the Crest of the Wave*, says, "I have before me a recent list of openings in a...mission agency which will go unnamed. Of fifty different categories, only two relate to evangelism, both focused on youth. The rest of the categories include, among others, agronomists, music teachers, nurses, automobile mechanics, secretaries, electronics professors, and ecologists."[1]

Although in the early days of our mission I had thought of raising money for orphans and relief operations, I now decided to drop those programs. Others were doing a far better job than we ever could in that area. Besides, it seemed to me the local church, rather than the missionary, should become the center of the outreach.

Social concern *is* a natural fruit of the gospel. But to put it first is to put the cart before the horse; and from experience, we have seen it fail in India for over two hundred years.

So I made a big decision. I decided to get involved only in preaching the gospel and make church planting the central concern of our work. I didn't go this route because I felt other Christian charities and ministries of compassion were wrong in showing the love of Christ, but because I felt we needed to bring the balance back. With so many concentrating on social work, I decided to get involved where there was obviously the greatest need.

But I didn't publicly tell anyone about my decision. I knew this subject would be controversial, and I was afraid others would think I was being judgmental. Most of all, I was afraid people would label me a "fighting fundy" reactionary. I didn't want to appear like a fanatic. All I wanted to do was help the native missionary movement, and I reasoned that getting into an argument over mission strategy wasn't the way to do it.

Then came Victoria, Texas.

The presentation was going nicely. I had shown the GFA slides and was making an impassioned plea for our work. I explained the philosophy of our ministry — giving the biblical reasons why the heathen are lost unless native missionaries go to them.

Suddenly, I felt the Spirit prompting me to talk about the dangers of the humanist social gospel. No one in the audience knew the agony I was going through. I paused for the briefest moment, then went on without saying anything about that subject. I just didn't have the courage to speak about it in public. What would people think? If I spoke out, I'd make enemies everywhere. I knew you couldn't find a church or mission in America which didn't have some kind of social work going. People wouldn't understand. They'd think I didn't care about the hungry, naked, needy and suffering.

Why, I asked myself, should I make waves? People will think I'm an unloving fool — a spoiler of other Christian work. So I managed to get through my presentation, and feeling relieved, I opened up the meeting to questions.

But the Holy Spirit was not about to let me off the hook.

From far in the back of the room a tall man — at least "six foot three," as they say in Texas — came walking steadily up the aisle. He looked bigger and bigger as he came closer to me. I didn't know who he was or what he had to say, but somehow I felt instinctively that God had sent him.

Wrapping a huge arm around my skinny shoulders, he said some words I still can hear ringing today: "This man here, our brother, is fearful and afraid to speak the truth...and he's struggling with it."

I felt my face and neck getting hot with guilt. How did this big cowboy know that? But it got worse, and I was about to see proof that the Spirit of the living God was really using this tall Texan to deliver a powerful confirmation and rebuke to me.

He went on, "The Lord has led you in ways others have not walked and shown you things others have not seen. The souls of millions are at stake. You must speak the truth about the misplaced priority on the mission field. You must call the body of Christ to return to the task of preaching salvation and snatching souls from hell."

I felt like a zero. My worst fears had come upon me, and yet this was undeniably a miraculous prophecy inspired by God — confirming both my disobedience and the very message God had called me to preach fearlessly. But my humiliation and liberation weren't over yet. "The Lord has asked me," he said, "to call the elders up here to pray for you that this fear of man will leave you."

Suddenly I felt like even less than a zero. I had been first introduced, I thought, as a great mission leader. Now I felt like a little lamb. I wanted to defend myself. I didn't feel as if I were being controlled by a spirit of fear; I had felt that I was just acting logically to protect the interests of our mission. But I submitted anyway, feeling a little ridiculous.

Soon the elders of the congregation were crowding around me to pray for an anointing of power on my preaching ministry. And something happened. I felt that power of God envelop me.

A few minutes later I got up from my knees as a changed man. I was released from the bondage of fear that had gripped me. All doubts were gone. I knew God had placed a burden on my life to deliver this message.

Since that day I've insisted we recover the genuine gospel of Jesus — that balanced New Testament message which begins not with the fleshly and worldly needs of people, but with the wisdom of God according to 1 Corinthians 1:30. The plan and wisdom of God are "born again" conversion that leads to righteousness, sanctification and redemption. Any "mission" that springs from "the base things of the world" is a betrayal of Christ and is what the Bible calls "another gospel." It cannot save or redeem people either as individuals or as a society. We preach a gospel, not for the years of time alone, but for eternity.

The only trouble with *half-truths* is that they contain within them *full lies*. Such is the case with this declaration issued at an international missionary conference: "Our fathers were impressed with the horror that men should die without Christ; we were equally impressed with the horror that they should live without Christ."

Out of such rhetoric — usually delivered passionately by an ever-growing number of sincere humanists within our churches — come myriads of worldly social programs. Such efforts really snatch salvation and true redemption from the poor — condemning them to eternity in hell.

Of course, there is a basic truth to the statement. Living this life without Christ is an existence of horrible emptiness, one which offers no hope or meaning. But the subtle humanist lie it hides places the accent on the welfare of this present physical life.

What few realize is that this teaching grew out of the influence of nineteenth-century humanists, the very same men who gave us modern atheism, communism and the many other modern philosophies that deny God's sovereignty in the affairs of men. They are, as the Bible says, "anti-Christs."

Modern man unconsciously holds highest the humanistic ideals of happiness, freedom, and economic, cultural and social progress for all mankind. This secular view says there is no God, heaven or hell; just one chance at life, so do what makes you most happy. They also teach that "since all men are brothers," we should work for that which contributes toward the welfare of all men.

This teaching — so attractive on the surface — has entered our churches in many ways. It has created a man-centered and man-made gospel based on changing the outside and social status of man by meeting his physical needs. The cost is his eternal soul.

The so-called humanist gospel — which isn't really the "good news" at all — is called by many names. Sometimes it is argued for in familiar biblical and theological terms; sometimes in English it is called the "social gospel" or the "holistic gospel," but the label isn't important.

You can tell the humanist gospel because it refuses to admit that the basic problem of humanity is not physical, but spiritual. *The humanist won't tell you sin is the root cause of all human suffering.* The latest emphasis of the movement starts by arguing that we should operate mission outreach that provides "care for the whole man," but it ends up providing help for only the body and soul — ignoring the spirit.

Because of this teaching, many churches and mission societies now are redirecting their limited outreach funds and personnel away from evangelism to something vaguely called "social concern." Today the majority of Christian missionaries find themselves primarily involved in feeding the hungry, caring for the sick through hospitals, housing the homeless, or other kinds of relief and development work.

In extreme cases, the logical direction of this thinking can lead to organizing guerrilla forces, planting terrorist bombs, or less extreme activities like sponsoring dance and aerobic exercise classes. This is done in the name of Jesus and supposedly is based on His command to go into all the world and preach the gospel to every creature. The mission of the church, as defined by these humanists, can be almost anything except winning people to Christ and discipling them.

History already has taught us that this gospel — without the blood of Christ, conversion and the cross — is a total failure. It seldom positively affects the very social condition upon which it primarily focuses. In China and India we have had seven generations of this teaching. It was brought to us by the British missionaries in a slightly different form in the middle of the last century. My people have watched the English hospitals and schools come and go without any noticeable effect on either our churches or society.

Watchman Nee, an early Chinese native missionary, already had put his finger on the problem in a series of lectures delivered in the years before World War II. Listen to some of his comments on such efforts as recorded in the book *Love Not the World*:

> When material things are under spiritual control they fulfill their proper subordinate role. Released from that restraint they manifest very quickly the power that lies behind them. The law of their nature asserts itself, and their worldly character is proved

by the course they take.

The spread of missionary enterprise in our present era gives us an opportunity to test this principle in the religious institutions of our day and of our land. Over a century ago the Church set out to establish in China schools and hospitals with a definite spiritual tone and an evangelistic objective. In those early days not much importance was attached to the buildings, while considerable emphasis was placed on the institutions' role in the proclamation of the Gospel. Ten or fifteen years ago you could go over the same ground and in many places find much larger and finer institutions on those original sites, but compared with the earlier years, far fewer converts. And by today many of those splendid schools and colleges have become purely educational centers, lacking in any truly evangelistic motive at all, while to an almost equal extent, many of the hospitals exist now solely as places merely of physical and no longer spiritual healing. The men who initiated them had, by their close walk with God, held those institutions steadfastly into His purpose; but when they passed away, the institutions themselves quickly gravitated toward worldly standards and goals, and in doing so classified themselves as "things of the world." We should not be surprised that this is so.

Nee continues to expand on the theme, this time addressing the problem of emergency relief efforts for the suffering:

In the early chapters of the Acts we read how a contingency arose which led the Church to institute relief for the poorer saints. That urgent institution of social service was clearly blessed of God, but it was of a temporary nature. Do you exclaim, "How good if it had continued?" Only one who does not know God would say that. Had those relief measures been prolonged indefinitely they would certainly have veered in the direction of the world, once the spiritual influence at work in their inception was removed. It is inevitable.

For there is a distinction between the Church of God's building, on the one hand, and on the other, those valuable social and charitable by-products that are thrown off by it from time to time through the faith and vision of its members. The latter, for all their origin in spiritual vision, possess in themselves a power of independent survival which the Church of God does not have. They are works which the faith of God's children may initiate and pioneer, but which once the way has been shown and the professional standard set, can be readily sustained or imitated by men of the world quite apart from that faith.

The Church of God, let me repeat, never ceases to be dependent upon the life of God for its maintenance.[2]

The trouble with the social gospel, even when it is clothed in religious garb and operating within Christian institutions, is that it seeks to fight what is basically a spiritual warfare with weapons of the flesh.

Our battle is not against flesh and blood or symptoms of sin like poverty and sickness. It is against Lucifer and countless demons who struggle day and night to take human souls into a Christless eternity.

As much as we want to see hundreds and thousands of new missionaries go into all the dark places, if they don't know what

110

they are really there for — and what they must do — the result will be fatal. We must send soldiers into battle with the right weapons and understanding of the enemy's tactics.

If we intend to answer man's greatest problem — his separation from the eternal God — with rice handouts, then we are throwing a drowning man a board instead of helping him out of the water.

A spiritual battle fought with spiritual weapons will produce eternal victories. This is why we insist upon restoring a right balance to gospel outreach. The accent must first and always be on evangelism and discipleship.

12

A Bowl of Rice No Substitute
for the Holy Spirit

To keep Christian missions off balance, Satan has woven a masterful web of deceit and lies. He has invented a whole system of appealing half-truths to confuse the church and ensure that millions will go to hell without ever receiving the gospel. Here are a few of his more common inventions:

Lie number one: *How can we preach the gospel to a man with an empty stomach?*

The result of this lie is the fact that, during the last hundred years, the majority of the mission money has been invested in social work. Evangelism and church planting have been ignored and neglected. While it appears to be a rational and logical statement, I disagree with it. A man's stomach has nothing to do with his heart's condition of being a rebel against the holy God.

A rich American on Fifth Avenue in New York City or a poor beggar on the streets of Bombay are both rebels against God almighty, according to the Bible. For all people, the only way to become a child of God and inherit His kingdom is to repent from sin and humble ourselves before the Lord.

Lie number two: *Humanitarian work is mission work.*

This lie is the tragedy of all tragedies. It is one of the most serious misunderstandings of all time. It has caused millions to die and go to hell without hearing the real gospel of Christ. This lie is taught and spread almost daily in TV specials and mail-outs, as Christian organizations ask for funds to meet only the physical needs of man.

The average church member unthinkingly drops a few dollars in the mission offering plate, trusting that the missionaries "out there" are involved in saving the 2.7 billion unreached souls. But in most cases, he or she is being horribly deceived. With all their social efforts, such mission representatives are simply making a doomed man feel a little better before he goes out into an eternity of suffering.

Lie number three: *Social work is not only mission work, but it is equal to preaching.*

Death and the grave are in this statement. Luke 16:9-23 tells us the pitiful story of the rich man and Lazarus. Of what benefit were the possessions of the rich man? He could not pay his way out of hell. His riches could not comfort him. The rich man had lost everything including his soul. What about Lazarus? He didn't have any possessions to lose, but he had made preparations for his soul. What was more important during their time on earth? Was it the care for the "body temple" or the immortal soul? "For what does it profit a man if he shall gain the whole world and lose his own soul?" (Luke 9:25).

It is a crime against lost humanity to go in the name of Christ and missions *just* to do the social work and yet neglect calling men to repent — to give up their idols and rebellion — following Christ with all their heart. Lie number four: *They will not listen to the gospel unless we offer them something else first.*

I have sat on the streets of Bombay with beggars — poor men who very soon would die. In sharing the gospel with many of them, I told them I had no material goods to give them, but I came to offer eternal life. I began to share the love of Jesus who died for their souls, about the many mansions in my Father's house (John 14:1-2) and the fact that they can go there to hunger and thirst no more. The Lord Jesus will wipe away every tear from their eyes, I said. They shall no longer be in any debt. There shall no longer be any mourning, or crying or pain (Rev. 7:16; 21:4).

And what a joy it was to see some of them opening their hearts after hearing about the forgiveness of sin they can find in Jesus. That is exactly what the Bible teaches in Romans 10:17, "Faith cometh by hearing, and hearing by the Word of God."

Many times I have given my clothes, food and money to poor people. But I never gave any of those things away with the hope this was going to make them come to Jesus Christ or give them the desire to repent. And neither did Jesus. He helped the poor because He loved them; but He spent most of His ministry teaching and making disciples.

It is impossible to substitute a bowl of rice for the Holy Spirit and the Word of God and then expect the same results. This never saves a soul and rarely changes the attitude of a man's heart. Anyone who has ever done social work will explain to you what I mean. Even Jesus rebuked the multitude because He knew their hearts. Many followed Him only as long as it looked as if they'd get a free lunch.

I am not saying the rich churches of America shouldn't continue to spend billions of dollars to meet human needs both here and abroad; yet we must realize we won't even begin to make a dent in the kingdom of darkness until we lift up Christ with all the authority, power and revelation that is given to us in the Bible.

I first learned this horrible truth about the ineffectiveness of humanitarian aid in the late 1970s at a North India survey expedition before we first went to preach. Throughout the Indian churches, the various mission hospitals and schools of North India are well-known.

My co-workers and I eagerly looked forward to visiting some of these missionaries and seeing the local churches. We especially wanted to meet the believers in the villages near these famed mission stations.

To our amazement we could not find a living congregation anywhere. There were hardly any believers at all. The surrounding villages were as deep in spiritual darkness as they had been two hundred years ago before the missionaries came. We were

114

shocked to find after eighty to one hundred years of constant mission work, and after an investment of millions of dollars in these areas, few, if any, living, New Testament churches existed.

As I have traveled throughout India and many other Asian nations, I have seen this same scenario repeated over and over.

In few countries is the failure of Christian humanism more apparent than in Thailand. There, after 150 years of showing marvelous social compassion, the church still makes up only one-tenth of one percent of the entire population.

Self-sacrificing missionaries probably have done more to modernize the country than any other single force. They gave the country the core of its civil service, education and medical systems.

Working closely with the royal family, the missionaries played the crucial role in eliminating slavery and keeping the country free of Western control during the colonial era.

Thailand owes to missionaries its widespread literacy, first printing press, first university, first hospital, first doctor and almost every other benefit of education and science. In every area, including trade and diplomacy, Christian missionaries put the needs of the host nation first and helped usher in the twentieth century.

But today virtually all that remains of this is a shell of good works.

Millions have meanwhile slipped into eternity without the Lord. They died more educated, better governed and healthier — but they still died without Christ and are bound for hell.

Many questions about this disaster started to hurt me deeply. I asked myself, What went wrong? Were these missionaries not dedicated enough? Were their doctrines unscriptural? Perhaps they did not believe in eternal hell or eternal heaven. Did they lack Bible training, or did they just not go out to preach to the lost? Did they shift their priorities from being interested in saving souls to relieving human suffering? I know now it was probably a little of all of these things.

While I was seeking answers, I met poor native brothers involved in gospel work in pioneer areas. They had nothing material to offer the people to whom they preached — no agricultural training and no medical relief or school program. In fact, some of them had very little formal education themselves. But I found that hundreds of souls got saved. In a few years, a number of churches were established.

Again I asked myself, What are these brothers doing right to have these kinds of results, while the other groups with many more advantages had failed?

I finally came to the conclusion that the answer lies in our basic understanding of what mission work is all about. There is nothing wrong with charitable acts — but they are not to be confused with preaching the gospel.

Feeding programs can save a man dying from hunger. Medical aid can prolong life and fight disease. Housing projects can make this temporary life more comfortable — but only the gospel of Jesus Christ can save a soul from a life of sin and an eternity in hell!

Sin is the root cause of the world's suffering. The battle against hunger and poverty is a spiritual battle, not a physical or social one. The only weapon that will ultimately win the fight is the gospel of Jesus Christ.

To look into the sad eyes of a hungry child or see the wasted life of a drug addict is only to see the evidence of Satan's hold on this world. He is the ultimate enemy of mankind, and he will do everything within his considerable power to kill and destroy people. But to try to fight this terrible enemy with physical weapons is like fighting tanks with stones.

When commerce had been established with the Fiji islanders, a merchant who was an atheist and skeptic landed on the island to do business. He was talking to the Fiji chief and noticed a Bible and some other paraphernalia of religion around the house.

"What a shame," he said, "that you have listened to this foolish nonsense of the missionaries."

The chief replied, "Do you see the large white stone over

there? That is a stone where just a few years ago we used to smash the heads of our victims to get at their brains. Do you see that large oven over there? That is the oven where just a few years ago we used to bake the bodies of our victims before we feasted upon them. Had we not listened to what you call the nonsense of those missionaries, I assure you that your head would already be smashed on that rock and your body would be baking in that oven."

There's no record of the merchant's response to that explanation of the importance of the gospel of Christ.

When God changes the heart and spirit, then the physical changes also. To anyone who wants to get involved in meeting the needs of the poor in this world, there's no better place to start than by preaching the gospel. It has done more to lift up the downtrodden, the hungry and the needy than all the social programs ever imagined by secular humanists.

Recently the World Bank published a report revealing for the first time that twenty-seven million Chinese starved to death during the "Great Leap Forward" economic development scheme of Mao Tse-Tung in the 1950s. More recently the same thinking led to the deaths of three million Cambodians when the communists took over Kampuchea. Let us never forget that these schemes — plus the actions of all the Hitlers and Stalins in this century — have been the logical extension of secular humanism applied to government. This is the best these social engineers have to offer when they have total control of a nation. We need to ponder long and hard the devastating results this same thinking has had on the church and its mission to a lost world. Could it be that millions are suffering the flames of hell today because we focused on meeting superficial physical needs rather than concentrating on their most basic need?

If the pure gospel had been preached in China and India in the last century — instead of a watered-down version of the Sermon on the Mount — I'm sure that freedom and prosperity would prevail over much of Asia today. Indirectly, the real gospel produces more social change than all the efforts of the world combined. The various humanist gospels are really mankind's pitiful efforts to find a shortcut to heaven while still on this earth.

But we cannot change the past; we must concentrate on preaching the true gospel of Christ to our generation. A.W. Tozer said it well in his book *Of God and Man*: "To spread an effete, degenerate brand of Christianity to pagan lands is not to fulfill the commandment of Christ or discharge our obligation to the heathen."[1]

These terrible words of Jesus should haunt our souls: "Ye compass sea and land to make one proselyte and when he is made, ye make him twofold more the child of hell than yourself" (Matt. 23:15).

We must learn from the past mistakes of missions and not repeat them. Just before China was taken over by the communists, one communist officer, talking to a missionary named John Meadow, made this revealing statement: "You missionaries have been in China for over a hundred years, but you have not won China to your cause. You lament the fact that there are uncounted millions who have never heard the name of your God. Nor do they know anything of your Christianity. But we communists have been in China less than ten years, and there is not a Chinese who does not know...has not heard the name of Stalin...or something of communism.

"What missionaries have failed to do in a hundred years, we communists have done in ten. We have filled China with our doctrine.

"Now let me tell you why you have failed and we have succeeded," the officer continued. "You have tried to win the attention of masses by building churches, missions, mission hospitals, schools and what not. But we communists have printed our message and spread our literature all over China.

"Someday we will drive you missionaries out of our country, and we will do it by the means of the printed page."

Today, of course, John Meadow is out of China. The communists were true to their word. They won China and drove out the missionaries. Indeed, what missionaries failed to do in a hundred years, the communists did in ten. One Christian leader said that if the church had spent as much time on preaching the gospel as it did on hospitals, orphanages, schools and rest homes — needful though they were — the bamboo curtain would not exist today.

The tragedy of China is being repeated today in other countries. When we allow a mission activity to focus on the physical needs of man without the correct spiritual balance, we are participating in a program that ultimately sends people to hell.

13

He Didn't Want Fans
but Disciples

If we could spend only one minute in the flames and torment of hell, we would see how really unloving is the so-called gospel that prevails in much of missions today.

Theology, which is only a fancy word for what we believe, makes all the difference on the mission field. When we go to the book of Acts, we find that these disciples were totally convinced about the lostness of man without Christ. Not even persecution could stop them from calling people everywhere to repent and turn to Christ.

Paul cries out in Romans 10:9-15 for the urgency of preaching Christ. In his day, the social and economic problems in cities like Corinth and Ephesus and other places were the same or worse than those we face today. Yet the apostles did not set out to establish social relief centers, hospitals or educational institutions. Paul declared in 1 Corinthians 2:2, "When I came to you,...I determined not to know anything among you save Jesus Christ and him crucified."

Paul recognized that Jesus Christ was the ultimate answer to all man's problems. While he was concerned about the poor saints, you cannot miss the primary emphasis of his life and message.

I have spoken in churches which had millions of dollars invested in buildings — churches with pastors known as excellent

Bible teachers with a heart of love for people. Yet I have discovered that many of them have absolutely no missionary program of any kind.

In preaching to one of these churches, I made the following statement: "While you claim to be evangelicals and pour time and life into learning more and more biblical truths, in all honesty, I do not think you believe the Bible."

They were shocked. But I continued.

"If you believed the Bible you say you believe, the very knowledge there is a real place called hell — where millions will go and spend eternity if they die without Christ — would make you the most desperate people in the world to give up everything you have to keep missions and reaching the lost as your top priority."

The problem with this congregation, as with many today, is that they didn't believe in hell. Yet, all through the Bible, there it is. It is mentioned, in fact, more often than heaven. Yet how we Christians struggle with it.

C.S. Lewis, that great British defender of the faith, wrote, "There is no doctrine which I would more willingly remove from Christianity than this (hell). I would pay any price to be able to say truthfully, 'All will be saved.' "

But Lewis, like us, realized that was neither truthful nor within his power to change.

Jesus Himself often spoke of hell and coming judgment. The Bible calls it the place of unquenchable fire, where the worms which eat the flesh don't die — a place of outer darkness where there is eternal weeping and gnashing of teeth.

These and hundreds of other verses tell of a real place where lost man will spend eternity if he dies without Jesus Christ.

Only a very few believers seem to have integrated the reality of hell into their life-style. In fact, it is difficult to feel that our friends who don't know Jesus really are destined to eternal hell.

Many Christians hold within their hearts the idea that, somehow or other, ways of redemption are available to those who have not heard. But the Bible doesn't give us a shred of hope for such a belief. It states clearly that it is "appointed unto men once to die, but after this the judgment" (Heb. 9:27).

There is no way out of death, hell, sin and the grave except Jesus Christ. He said, "I am the way, the truth, and the life: no man cometh unto the Father, but by me" (John 14:6).

How different our churches would be if we started to live by the true revelation of the Word of God about hell. Instead, missions, both in the West and in the East, have been infected with death and continue to pass out death to the millions of lost souls who surround us.

The church Jesus called out of this world to be separated unto Himself has, to a great extent, forgotten her reason for existence. Her loss of balance is seen in the current absence of holiness, spiritual reality and concern for the lost. Substituted for the life she once knew are teaching and reaching for prosperity, pleasure, politics and social involvement.

"Evangelical Christianity," commented Tozer prophetically before his death, "is now tragically below the New Testament standard. Worldliness is an accepted fact of our way of life. Our religious mood is social instead of spiritual."

The further our leaders wander from the Lord, the more they turn to the ways of the world. One church in Dallas recently spent several million dollars to construct a gymnasium "to keep our young people interested in church." Many churches have become like secular clubs with softball teams, golf lessons, schools and exercise classes to keep people coming to their buildings and giving them their tithes. Some churches have gone so far from the Lord that they sponsor yoga and meditation courses — Western adaptations of Hindu religious exercises.

If this is what is considered mission outreach at home, is it any wonder the same churches fall prey to the seductive philosophy of Christian humanists when planning overseas missionary work?

Real Christian mission always is aware there is eternal hell to shun and heaven to gain. We need to restore the balanced vision

General William Booth had when he started the Salvation Army. He had an unbelievable compassion for winning lost souls to Christ. His own words tell the story of what he envisioned for the movement: "Go for souls, and go for the worst."

What would Jesus do if He walked today into our churches?

I am afraid He would not be able to say to us: "You have kept the faith, you have run the race without turning left or right, and you have obeyed My command to reach this world."

I believe He would go out to look for a whip, because we have made His Father's house a den of robbers. If that is so, then we must recognize that the hour is too desperate for us to continue to deceive ourselves. We are past the point of revival or reformation. If this gospel is to be preached in all the world in our lifetime, we must have a Christian, heaven-sent revolution.

But before revolution can come, we must recognize the need for one. We are like a lost man looking at a road map. Before we can choose the right road that takes us to our destination, we must determine where we went wrong, go back to that point and start over. So my cry to the body of Christ is simple: Turn back to the true gospel road. We need to preach again the whole counsel of God. Our priority must again be placed on calling men to repentance and snatching them from hell-fire.

Time is short. If we are not willing to plead in prayer for a mission revolution — and let it start in our own personal lives, homes and churches — we will lose this generation to Satan.

We can go trading souls for bodies, or we can make a difference by sponsoring Bible-believing native missionaries overseas.

In 1983, forty Indian villages, once considered Christian, turned back to Hinduism. Could it be that whole villages which had experienced the liberating gospel of Jesus Christ would turn back into the bondage of Satan?

No. These villages were called "Christian" only because they had been "converted" by missionaries who used hospitals, material goods and other incentives to attract them to Christianity. But when the material rewards were reduced — or when other competing movements offered similar benefits — these converts reverted to their old cultural ways. In missionary terms, they were "rice Christians."

When "rice" was offered, they changed their names and their religions, responding to the "rice." But they never understood the true gospel of the Bible. After all the effort, these people were as lost as ever. But now they were even worse off — they were presented a completely wrong picture of what it means and what it takes to follow Christ.

Could that be what we fear in North America: no gyms — no softball teams — no converts?

The lesson from the mission field is that meeting physical needs alone does not get people to follow God. Whether hungry or full, rich or poor, human beings remain in rebellion against God without the power of the gospel.

Unless we return to the biblical balance — to the gospel of Jesus as He proclaimed it — we'll never be able to put the accent where it rightly belongs in the outreach mission of the church.

Jesus was compassionate to human beings as total persons. He did all He could to help them, but He never forgot the main purpose of His earthly mission: to reconcile men to God, to die for sinners and redeem their souls from hell. Jesus cared for the spiritual side of man first, then the body.

This is illustrated clearly in Matthew 9:2-7 when He first forgave the sins of the paralytic then healed his body.

In John 6:1-13, Jesus miraculously fed five thousand hungry men plus women and children. He fed them *after* he preached, not *before* to attract their attention.

Later, in verse 26, we find that these people followed Jesus not because of His teachings, or who He was, but because He had fed them. They even tried to make Him king for the wrong reason. Seeing the danger of their spiritual misunderstanding, Jesus withdrew from them. He didn't want fans but disciples.

The apostles did not fear to tell the beggar that "silver and gold have I none; but such as I have give I thee" (Acts 3:6). Then they preached the gospel.

I have had similar experiences all across India. I have yet to meet a person who was not willing to hear the wonderful news of Jesus because of his or her physical condition. Those who say otherwise are simply not telling the truth.

As Christians we must follow the example of Jesus. I do believe we must do all we can to relieve the pain and suffering around us. We must love our neighbors as ourselves in all areas of life. But we must keep supreme the priority of sharing the message of salvation to them — and we must never minister to the physical needs at the expense of preaching Christ. This is biblical balance, the true gospel of Jesus.

14

Without Christ
People Serve Demon Spirits

My hosts in the Southern city where I was preaching at a mission conference had thoughtfully booked me into a motel room. It was good to have a few minutes alone, and I looked forward to having some time for prayer and Scripture meditation.

While settling in, I flipped on the big TV set that dominated the room.

What burst on the screen shocked me more than anything I had ever seen in America. There in beautiful color was an attractive woman seated in the lotus position teaching yoga. I watched in horror and amazement as she praised the health benefits of the breathing techniques and other exercises of this Eastern religious practice. What her viewers did not know is that yoga is designed for one purpose only — to open up the mind and body to receive visitations from demon spirits.

Because this American yogi was dressed in a chic Danskin body suit, claimed a Ph.D. degree and was on educational TV, I assume many of the viewers were deceived into believing this was just another harmless exercise show. But those of us born and raised in nations dominated by the power of darkness know better. Hundreds of Eastern religions are marketing themselves in the United States and Canada under innocuous — even scientific-sounding — brand names.

Few Westerners, when they see news reports of the poverty, suffering and violence in Asia, take time to stop and ask why.

How is it that the East is bound into an endless cycle of suffering while Western nations are so blessed? Secular humanists are quick to reel out many historic and pseudo-scientific reasons for the disparity, because they are unwilling to face the truth. But the real reason is simple: The Judeo-Christian heritage of Europe has brought the favor of God, while false religions have brought the curse of Babylon on all the nations of Asia.

Mature Christians realize the Bible teaches there are only two religions in this world. There is the worship of the one true God, and there is a false system of demonic alternative invented in ancient Iran. From there, Persian armies and priests spread their faith to India where it took root. Hindu missionaries in turn spread it throughout the rest of Asia. Animism, Buddhism and all other Asian religions have a common heritage in this one religious system.

Because many Westerners are unaware of this fact, demonic influences now are able to spread Eastern mysticism in the West through pop culture, rock bands, singers and even university professors. The media have become the new vehicle for the spread of demon worship and idolatry by American gurus.

But it is hard to blame the average Christian for misunderstanding what is happening to them and the Judeo-Christian heritage which has brought such blessings on their land. Most have never taken the time to study and discern the real situation in the Orient. Few pastors or prophets are sounding the alarm.

In Asia the religion of Babylon is woven into every waking minute of the day. Without Christ, people live to serve demon spirits. Religion relates to everything including your name, birth, education, marriage, business deals, contracts, travel and death.

Because Oriental culture and religion are a mystery, many people in the West are fascinated by it without knowing the power of these demons to blind and enslave their followers. What routinely follows the mystery religions of Babylon is degradation, humiliation, poverty and suffering — even death.

Most believers in America, I find, are overwhelmed by the TV and media news reports from Asia. The numbers reported are beyond imagination: people, problems and needs. The injustice, poverty, suffering and violence appear to be unstoppable. All things Oriental appear to be mysterious. Everything, it seems, is measured either on a grand scale or by one so different that it can't be compared to things familiar.

So in all my travels, I have found it is extremely difficult for most people to relate to Asia's needs. Sometimes I wish I could just scoop up my audience and take them on a six-month tour of Asia. But since that's not possible, I must use words, pictures, slides and video films to paint a clearer picture. It is important that we take the time to understand the real need.

Although Asia is admittedly hard to understand, we must not let that be a reason to ignore it. Two out of every three people in the world live there. That's more than the combined populations of all the African and Latin American mission fields combined. (In fact, it's more than the combined populations of Europe, Africa, North America and South America.)

In terms of numbers alone, Asia must be the top priority in Christian evangelism. From the standpoint of Christian missions, these are more than just big numbers. Asia makes up the vast majority of 2.7 billion hidden peoples who are being missed by traditional missionary efforts and mass media evangelism. They are *the most lost of the lost* — trapped in utter spiritual darkness.

But the big question I hear almost daily is, How can we help— is there anything we can do with problems so gigantic?

As I travel all over North America sharing the needs of missions in Asia, I find that Christians are hungry for straight answers. They want to help if they only knew how.

What are the challenges facing native missions today? How real are the needs? How can Christians best help the Asian church and its missionary efforts?

While I am not trying to minimize the social and material needs of the Asian nations, it is important to realize that Asia's basic problem is a spiritual one. This is easy to lose sight of when the Western media focuses almost entirely on our problems of hunger, poverty and violence. It is difficult for Americans to see pictures of all those starving children on TV without getting the false impression that hunger is the biggest problem.

But what causes the hunger? We as Christians know these horrible conditions are only symptoms of the real problem — spiritual bondage to satanic philosophies. The key factor — and the most neglected — in understanding India's hunger problem is the belief of Hinduism and its effect on food production. Most people know of the "sacred cows" that roam free, eating tons of grain while nearby people starve. But a lesser known and more sinister culprit is another animal protected by religious belief — the rat.

According to those who believe in reincarnation, the rat must be protected as a likely recipient for a reincarnated soul on its way up the ladder of spiritual evolution to Nirvana. Though many reject this and seek to poison rats, large scale efforts of extermination have been thwarted by religious outcry. As one of India's statesmen has said, "India's problems will never cease until her religion changes."

Rats eat or spoil 20 percent of India's food grain every year. A study of United Nations statistics by *India Journal*[1] found that food grain losses in hot, moist climates could be as high as 40 percent from loss due to rodents, birds, insects and spoilage resulting from poor storage. The chief culprit is the Bengal bandicoot rat. A recent survey in the wheat-growing district of Hapur in North India revealed there is an average of ten rats per house.

Of the 1982 harvest of cereals in India, including maize, wheat, rice, millet and so on — a total of 134 million metric tons — the 20 percent loss from rats amounted to 26.8 million metric tons.

The picture becomes more comprehensible by imagining a train of boxcars carrying that amount of grain. With each car holding about eighty-two metric tons, the train would contain 327,000 cars and stretch for 3,097 miles. The annual food grain loss in India would fill a train longer than the distance between New York and Los Angeles.

From these statistics it is apparent that India produces enough food to feed its nearly one billion people. Social programs and attempts to meet physical needs will never get to the root of the problem. Preaching of the gospel does.

The devastating effects of the rat in India should make it an object of scorn. Instead, because of the spiritual blindness of the people, the rat is protected and in some places even worshipped.

Thirty miles south of Bikaner in North India is a temple where rats are worshipped, according to an article in the *India Express.*

"Hundreds of rats, called 'kabas' by the devotees, scurry around merrily in the large compound of the temple and sometimes even around the image of the goddess Karni Devi situated in a cave. The rats are fed on prasad offered by the devotee or by the temple management. Legend has it that the fortunes of the community are linked to that of the rats.

"One has to walk cautiously through the temple compound; for if a rat is crushed to death, it is not only considered a bad omen but may also invite severe punishment. One is considered lucky if a rat climbs over one's shoulder. Better still to see a white rat."

Clearly, the agony we see in the faces of those starving children and beggars is actually caused by centuries of religious slavery. The single most important social reform that can be brought to Asia is the gospel of Jesus Christ. My people need the hope and truth that only the Lord Jesus can provide.

In my own beloved homeland of India, thousands of lives and billions of dollars go into social programs every year. Education, medical and relief efforts operate on a massive scale. It's fascinating for me to watch the seriousness with which U.S. politicians dramatically declare certain parts of their nation to be so-called disaster areas in times of natural calamity. Many of the crisis problems which are considered disasters here would be only normal, everyday living conditions in most of Asia. When we have disasters in the Orient, the death tolls read like Vietnam war body counts. Asian governments struggle with these tremendous social problems and limited resources.

Yet, despite all the massive social programs operating in India and other Asian countries, the problems of hunger, population and poverty continue to grow. The real culprit is not a person, lack of natural resources or a system of government. It is spiritual darkness. It thwarts every effort to make progress. It dooms our people to misery — both in this world and in the world to come.

That's why I declare our biggest need is spiritual. In India over three hundred million people have never heard the name of Jesus Christ mentioned even once.

Recently, for instance, one native missionary, who serves the Lord in Jammu, asked a shopkeeper on the market if he knew Jesus. After thinking a moment, he said, "Sir, I know everyone in our village. There is not one by that name who lives here. Why don't you go to the next village? He may live there."

Frequently native missionary evangelists find people who ask if Jesus is the brand name of a new soap or patent medicine. In India proper, there are nearly one billion people — three times the population of the United States. Only 3.5 percent of these call themselves Christians.* But almost all of the 0.4 percent of the population that is evangelical Christian is located in just two tiny regions. This is typical of all Asia. When there are born-again Christians, they usually are found huddled together in little pockets.

India, with nearly 500,000 unevangelized villages, is undoubtedly one of the greatest evangelistic challenges facing the world

---

* Although this figure reflects the official government census, a number of key Christian leaders who understand the situation believe the number of Christians is actually much greater than reported.

Christian community today. If present trends continue, it will soon be the world's most populous nation. While China has a greater need, there still is not the political freedom there that Indians now enjoy.

Many of India's twenty-two states have larger populations than whole nations in Europe and other parts of the world. Not only are our populations huge, but each state is usually as distinctive as if it were another world. Most have completely different cultures, dress, diet and languages. But few nations in Asia are homogenous. Most are like India to some extent; nations that are patchwork quilts of many languages, peoples and tribes. This diversity, in fact, is what makes Asia such a tremendous challenge to missionary work.

India, of course, isn't the only wide-open door for native missionaries. In nearly every nation there is some degree of freedom for evangelists who emerge from the local soil. Some of the most exciting right now are found in Korea, the Philippines and Thailand.

To give even a brief survey of all the opportunities would be a book in itself, but I would like to take a whirlwind tour of some of the more exciting open doors we are facing in the Third World today. Here is a country-by-country breakdown of just a few.

Afghanistan. Long one of the militantly anti-Christian nations in the world, this Marxist republic has been under martial law since 1978 when the Soviets invaded the country. The population, officially 99.3 percent Muslim, is constantly shifting as wars and civil strife continue. Many refugees have crossed the border into Pakistan, and there appear to be significant new opportunities to witness to them. There still is a death penalty for conversion to Christianity, however, and no Christian church ever has been established successfully inside the national borders. More than fifty-three languages are spoken by the twenty major ethnic groups.[2]

Bangladesh. One of the most densely populated in the world, this officially Muslim nation has been ruled by a military junta since 1975. Bengali, Urdu and English dominate the five major languages although thirty others are spoken. In the wake of the civil war that tore this nation from Pakistan in 1971, there have been several brief "open windows" of religious freedom. Among minority groups there has been considerable openness to Christ.[3]

Bhutan. This tiny Himalayan kingdom only recently experienced the first slight breezes of freedom. Still officially a Buddhist state, it was totally closed to any outside witness until 1965. It is illegal to evangelize, proselytize or worship publicly. Only three hundred Christians are estimated to exist among the 1.4 million population, but Indian believers living along the border or working in the country have many opportunities to share their faith. Landlocked, Bhutan depends totally on India for trade and foreign relations.[4]

Myanmar (formerly Burma). Although officially closed to outsiders since 1966, this intensely xenophobic nation does have a vigorous native missionary movement in the northern tribal areas. About 1.1 percent of the population is evangelical Protestant, one of the largest percentages in Asia. However, very few Burmese are believers. Most of the Christians are confined to tribal minorities such as the Shan and Karen. Buddhism is the semi-official but powerful religious force that seems to have a viselike grip on the Burmese. Politically, the nation is dominated by secular socialists — a totalitarian group controlled by the army. Although 70 percent of the population is Burmese, there are 129 minority people groups, including nearly one hundred tribes.[5]

Hong Kong. Gateway to China, this wealthy city-state has been a British Crown Colony since 1842. Soon to return to the control of China, it probably enjoys as much religious freedom as any nation in Asia. Over one hundred denominations flourish there among the 5.2 million population. Christians make up over 5 percent of the population, and this is the most vitally strategic city for Chinese evangelism.[6]

Indonesia. With one of the fastest-growing Christian communities in the world, this nation continues to be probably the greatest harvest field of Asia. More than 840 languages are spoken by the population of 151 million. Like Japan and the Philippines, it is made up of widely scattered islands. Complex and exciting, they contain scores of unreached people groups. Religious freedom is widespread, and recently there has been a remarkable outpouring of the Holy Spirit. Many are being called into village evangelism, and the three thousand islands promise to become one of the greatest growth areas for the native missionary movement.[7]

Japan. While religious freedom is protected by the government and many Western missionaries have struggled in this difficult field since World War II, the Japanese largely have refused to accept Christianity.

P.J. Johnstone describes the 118 million people of these islands as "...talented, materialistic, unresponsive and hidden in a centuries-old cocoon of culture and bondage to demonic powers and multiplied varieties of Buddhism."

Proud and apparently unable to respond to the gospel when preached by foreigners, the Japanese desperately need a native church and missionary movement. Evangelical believers make up only 0.03 percent of the population, but in spite of their small size, they have thrust out nearly two hundred missionaries to other Asian nations. The Japanese, if converted, could be a major force in carrying the gospel throughout Asia. Japan's legendary cultural, economic and educational achievements have turned it into one of the greatest nations on earth — and one of the greatest challenges to Christian missions in Asia.[8]

Korea. With probably the most dramatically Christian movement in the world, the Koreans have survived terrible persecution from both the communists and Japanese. They recently have experienced revivals and evangelistic movements throughout the church, government and military. Not only are Korean churches mushrooming, but native missionary movements are powerful forces both in the country and throughout Asia. Over six thousand Korean young people have pledged themselves to mission service in other Asian nations.[9]

Malaysia. Fiercely Muslim, the Malays themselves have vigorously and officially resisted the gospel. Missionary efforts by Westerners have practically stopped under rigid government restrictions. However, among the Chinese, Tamil Indians and the 170 tribal groups there has been steady evangelism and occasional revivals. The country's only hope to find Christ is in the raising up of a strong native evangelism movement internally.[10]

Maldives. Another Muslim stronghold, there are no known Christians on these islands located off the west coast of India. Only 155,000 people inhabit about 220 of the two thousand Maldivian Islands, and they represent an important evangelistic challenge to the Indian church. About ten thousand are living abroad in South India and Bombay.[11]

Nepal. Despite persecution, there are a growing number of Nepali Christians. Native missionaries are actively but covertly working in the country. About half the population is Nepali Hindus, the rest being various tribes and a large Indian minority. There are about nineteen ethno-linguistic groups in the nation.[12]

Despite recent changes in Nepal, still officially a Hindu nation, it is constitutionally illegal to change one's religion in this nation. As in many other Asian nations, believers in the Himalayan kingdom just north of India are discriminated against in school, on the job and in nearly every social activity. Two local Christians were recently beaten and imprisoned by government officials. Their crime? To write the word "Christian" on a government form that asked them to name their religion.

Pakistan. One of the most open doors in Asia, this Islamic republic of ninety-three million souls consistently has permitted Christian minorities a great deal of freedom, including the right to proclaim their faith. Ethnically, the country is almost 60 percent Punjabi but has nineteen major people groups. Muslims are more open than ever to listen to the gospel, and many fear the full imposition of Islamic law. Social pressures and the cultural unacceptability of the present Christian community are commonly pointed out as reasons for the lack of church growth. With the growing influx of Afghani refugees, there is even more reason to see a native missionary movement expand in this land.[13]

Philippines. With nearly 80 percent professing Roman Catholics, the Philippines is the only Asian nation that has claimed to be Christian. Over the last several years there has been a great spiritual move both within and outside the church. Many thousands are discovering real life in Jesus Christ, and evangelistic meetings attract large crowds everywhere. This archipelago of seven thousand islands offers one of the greatest spiritual opportunities in Asia today. Only a few hundred of the islands have a Christian witness. The evangelical population is less than 7 percent overall, and they are concentrated in one or two major cities. Ten languages and 150 dialects are spoken by the 173 separate people groups which make up this diverse nation of tiny islands.[14]

Singapore. Another city-state with vast potential as a sending base for native missionaries, it has been a secular state since 1965. Protestant evangelicals account for 1.7 percent of the population, considerably larger than in most Asian nations. Located in a group of forty-one small islands off the tip of Malaysia, the population of Singapore is 2.4 million, mostly crowded on the densely packed main island. The population is 75 percent Chinese, the rest being mostly Malay and Indians.[15]

Sri Lanka. A Buddhist, socialist republic off the southern coast of India, Sri Lanka generally is considered to be one of the worst evangelized countries in Asia. A succession of foreign invaders including the Portuguese, Dutch and British artificially imposed Christianity. The result has been deep anti-Christian bias and a revival of Buddhism in recent years. Fewer than fifty foreign missionaries now remain, and in a country torn by years of civil war a strong native missionary movement is absolutely essential if the nation is to be evangelized. The population of more than fifteen million is largely Singhalese with a large Tamil minority.[16]

Taiwan. Located off the coast of China, this island of sixteen million has a larger-than-average number of evangelicals, about

1.8 percent. After a period of great growth due to immigration —
and intense evangelism following the communist takeover of
mainland China — Taiwan churches have sent several hundred
native missionaries throughout Asia. As a sending nation, Taiwan
has significant potential.[17]

Thailand. Another hotbed of spiritual activity, this officially
Buddhist kingdom of thirty-five million is developing pockets of
great response to evangelistic activity. A vigorous native missionary movement is erupting, but church planting is limited mostly
to the Northeast. While less than 0.1 percent of the population is
evangelical, the current outreach is more fruitful than at any other
time in the history of the nation. Although the country is almost
80 percent Siamese Thai, there are thirty-six other major people
groups in the country. The major languages are Thai, English,
Lao, Chinese, Malay, Khmer, Vietnamese and fifty tribal dialects.[18]

15

Temples of This New Religion
Are Atomic Reactors

The native missionary movement, the only hope for these Asian nations, is not going unchallenged by either Satan or the world. Revivals of traditional religions such as Islam and Hinduism, the growth of secular materialism including communism, and the traditional cultural and nationalist barriers are all united in opposition to Christian mission activity.

Masih had terrible memories of his home and the persecution he had suffered there when he first turned to Christ while a Hindu priest. For years he had sought spiritual peace through self-discipline, yoga and meditation as required by his Brahmin caste.

He also had memories of rejection by his family because of his new faith and of the physical attacks when he refused to renounce Jesus. But God called, and so Masih returned to his home village in Uttar Pradesh, India.

"I was brought up in an orthodox Hindu home where we worshipped many gods," he says. "I even became the Hindu priest in our village, but I couldn't find the peace and joy I wanted.

"One day I received a gospel tract and read about the love of Jesus Christ. I answered the offer on the leaflet and enrolled in a correspondence course to learn more about Jesus.

"On January 1, 1978, I gave my life to Jesus Christ. I was baptized three months later and took the Christian name 'Masih' which means 'Christ.' "

138

For a Hindu, baptism and the taking of a Christian name symbolize a complete break with the pagan past. To avoid the censure which often comes with baptism, some wait years before they are baptized. But Masih didn't wait. The reaction was swift.

When his parents realized their son had rejected their Hindu gods, they began a campaign of persecution. To escape, Masih went to Kota in Rajasthan to search for a job.

For six months he worked in a factory and meanwhile joined a local group of believers. Through their encouragement, he enrolled in a Bible institute and began to master the Scriptures.

During his three years of study, he made his first trip home. "My father sent a telegram asking me to come home," Masih recalls. "He said he was 'terribly ill.' When I arrived, my family and friends asked me to renounce Christ. When I didn't, much persecution followed, and my life was in danger. I had to flee."

When he returned to school, Masih thought God would lead him to minister to some other part of India. He was shocked at the answer to his prayers.

"As I waited on the Lord, He guided me to go back and work among my own people," he says. "He wanted me to share the love of God through Christ with them, like the healed demoniac of Gadara whom He sent back to his own village."

Today, Ramkumar Masih — a former Hindu priest — is involved in church planting in his home city and surrounding villages. He is working alone among both Hindus and Muslims in a basically hostile environment.

Although Masih has not had to pay the ultimate price to win his people to Christ, every year a number of Christian missionaries and ordinary believers are killed for their faith throughout Asia. The total in this century probably numbers in the hundreds of thousands, undoubtedly more than the total number of Christians killed in the entire history of the church.

Revivals of traditional religions are occurring all over Asia. Although few countries have gone the route of Iran — where a religious revival of Islam actually toppled the state — religious factionalism is a major problem in many countries.

When government, media and educational institutions are taken over by atheistic materialists, there often can be a great backlash in most nations. As traditional religious leaders are finding out, it isn't enough to drive Western nations out. Secular humanists are in firm control of most Asian governments, and many traditional religious leaders miss the power they once exercised.

At the grass-roots level, traditional religion and nationalism often are deliberately confused and exploited by political leaders for short-term gain. In the villages, traditional religions still have a powerful hold on the minds of most people. Almost every village or community has a favorite idol or deity — there are 330 million gods in the Hindu pantheon alone. In addition, various animistic cults which involve the worship of powerful spirits are openly practiced alongside Islam, Hinduism and Buddhism.

In many areas the village temple still is the center of informal education, tourism and civic pride. Religion is big business, and temples take in vast sums of money annually.

Millions of priests and amateur practitioners of the occult arts also are profiteering from the continuation and expansion of traditional religions. Like the silversmiths in Ephesus, they aren't taking the spread of Christianity lightly. Religion, nationalism and economic gain mix as a volatile explosive that Satan uses to blind the eyes of millions.

But God is calling native missionaries to preach the gospel anyway, and many are taking the good news into areas solidly controlled by traditional religions.

But the enemies of the cross include more than just traditional religionists. A new force, even more powerful, is now sweeping across Asia. It is what the Bible calls the spirit of anti-Christ — the new religion of secular materialism. Often manifested as some form of communism, it has taken control of governments in a number of states including Afghanistan, Burma, Cambodia, China, Laos, North Korea, Tibet and Vietnam.

But in all Asian nations, even those with democracies like India and Japan, it has gained some control of the state in various non-communist forms.

The temples of this new religion are atomic reactors, oil refineries, hospitals and shopping malls. The priests are most often the technicians, scientists and military generals who are impatiently striving to rebuild the nations of Asia in the image of the industrial West.

The shift of political power in most of Asia has gone toward these men and women who promise health, peace and prosperity without a supernatural god — for man himself is their god.

In one sense, secular humanism and materialism correctly diagnose traditional religion as a major source of oppression and poverty throughout Asia. Humanism is a natural enemy of theistic religion because it is a worldly and scientific method to solve the problems of mankind without God.

As a result of this growing, scientific materialism, there are strong secularistic movements in every Asian nation. They unite and seek to eliminate the influence of all religion — including Christianity — from society.

Modern Asia, in the great cities and capitals where secular humanism reigns supreme, is controlled by many of the same drives and desires that have dominated the West for the last hundred years.

If traditional Asian religions represent an attack of the devil on Christianity, then secular humanism is an attack of the flesh. That leaves only one enemy to discuss, the anti-Christian pressure of the world.

This final barrier to Christ, and still probably the strongest of all, is the culture itself.

When Mahatma Gandhi returned to India from years of living in England and South Africa, he quickly realized the "Quit India" movement was failing because its national leadership was not willing to give up European ways. So even though he was Indian, he had to renounce his Western dress and customs or he would not have been able to lead his people out from under the British yoke. He spent the rest of his life relearning how to become an Indian again — in dress, food, culture and life-style. Eventually he gained acceptance by the common people of India. The rest is history. He became the father of my nation, the George Washington of modern India.

The same principle holds true of evangelistic and church planting efforts in all of Asia. We must learn to adapt to the culture. This is why the native evangelist, who comes from the native soil, is so effective. When Americans here in the United States are approached by yellow-robed Krishna worshippers — with their shaved heads and prayer beads — they reject Hinduism immediately. In the same way, Hindus reject Christianity when it comes in Western forms.

Have Asians rejected Christ? Not really. In most cases they have rejected only the trappings of Western culture that have fastened themselves onto the gospel. This is what the apostle Paul was referring to when he said he was willing to become "all things to all men" in order that he might win some.

When Asians share Christ with other Asians in a culturally acceptable way, the results are startling. One of the native missionaries we support in northwest India, for example, now has evangelized sixty villages and established thirty churches in a difficult area of the Punjab.

He has led hundreds to Christ. On a recent trip to India, I went out of my way to visit this man and his wife. I had to see for myself what kind of program he was using.

Imagine my surprise when I found he wasn't using any special technology at all — unless you want to call the motor scooter and tracts that we supplied "technology."

He was living just like the people. He had only a one-room house made of dung and mud. The kitchen was outside, also made of mud — the same stuff with which everything else is constructed in that region. To cook the food, his wife squatted in front of an open fire just like the neighboring women. What was so remarkable about this brother was that everything about him and his wife was so truly Indian. There was absolutely nothing foreign.

I asked Jager what kept him going in the midst of such

incredible challenge and suffering. He said, "Waiting upon the Lord, my brother."

I discovered he spent two to three hours daily in prayer, reading, and meditating on the Bible. This is what it takes to win Asia for Christ. This is the kind of missionary for which our nations cry out.

Jager was won to Christ by another native evangelist. This native preacher came and explained the living God to Jager while he was still a devout Hindu. He told him of a God who hates sin and became a man to die for sinners and set them free. This was the first time the gospel ever was preached in his village, and Jager followed the man around for several days.

Finally, he accepted Jesus as his Lord and was disowned by his family. Overjoyed and surprised by his newfound life, he went about distributing tracts from village to village, telling about Jesus. In the end, he sold his two shops. With the money he earned, he conducted evangelistic meetings in local villages.

This is a man of the culture, bringing Christ to his own people in culturally acceptable ways. The support we Asians need from the West, if we're to complete the work Christ has left us, must go to this kind of self-sacrificing missionary worker.

In light of the challenges facing missions in Asia today, what does this show us about the best possible methods to reach our people? I think the answer is obvious. We must recruit, equip and send out an army of native missionary evangelists.

Only native evangelists come prepared to meet the three big challenges we are now facing in the Orient.

First, they already understand the culture, customs and lifestyle as well as the language. They don't have to spend valuable time in lengthy preparations.

Second, the most effective communication occurs between peers. While there still may be social barriers to overcome, they are much smaller and more easily identified.

Third, it's a wiser investment of our resources because the native missionary works more economically than foreigners can.

One of the most basic laws of creation is that every living thing reproduces after its own kind. This fact applies in evangelism and discipleship, just as it does in other areas. If we are going to see a mass people movement to Christ, it will be done only through fielding many more thousands of native missionaries.

How many are needed? In India alone we still have 500,000 villages to reach. Looking at other nations, we realize thousands more remain without a witness. If we are to reach all the other hamlets open to us right now, Gospel for Asia will need additional native missionary evangelists by the tens of thousands. The cost to support this army will run into the millions annually. But this is only a fraction of the $4.8 billion U.S. churches lavished on their own needs and desires in 1986. The result will be a revolution of love that will bring millions of Asians to Christ.

The challenge of Asia cries out to us. The enemies of the cross abound. There are giants in the land, but none of them can stand against us as we move out in the authority and power of the Lord Jesus.

For the first time in history, by helping native evangelists it now is possible to see all of Asia evangelized in our generation. This is the bright side of the Asian situation. The problems we face are indeed great, but they can be overcome through a peaceful army of native missionary evangelists.

In spite of the opposition from traditional religion, secular materialism and long-standing cultural patterns, I am certain God wants us to unite with Christians around the world to raise up a Christian witness in every dark corner of Asia.

Part III

THE WAY

16

Offering the Water of Life
in a Foreign Cup

When we think about the awesome challenge of Asia, it is not too much to ask for a new army of missionaries to reach these nations for Christ. But we must ask ourselves: From where are we going to recruit them? Should we look for thousands of new Americans, Canadians and Western Europeans who will uproot themselves and their families to go overseas, learn the local languages and adopt an alien culture as their own? How will we get the governments of those lands to change their immigration and visa policies to let Western missionaries come in? Finally, how will we raise the additional billions of dollars that would be needed every year to keep those missionaries on the fields?

The answer is that tens of thousands of native missionaries are being raised up by the Lord in all these Third World nations right now. They are Asians. Many of them already live in the nation they must reach. Or they live in nearby cultures just a few hundred miles from the unevangelized villages to which they will be sent by the Lord.

The situation in world missions is depressing only when you think of it in terms of nineteenth-century Western colonialism.

If the actual task of world evangelization depends on the "sending of the white missionary," obeying the Great Commission truly becomes more impossible every day. But, praise God, the native missionary movement is growing, ready today to complete the task.

We are witnessing a new day in missions. This is the primary message I have for every Christian, pastor and mission leader. Just a few short years ago, no one dreamed the Asian church would be ready to lead the final thrust. But dedicated native evangelists are beginning to go out and reach their own.

And the exciting message I have for every believer is this: God is calling all of us to be part of what He is doing. *You have a role.*

We can make it possible for millions of brown and yellow feet to move out with the liberating gospel of Jesus. With the prayer and financial support of the Western church they can go preach the Word to the lost multitudes. The whole family of God is needed. Thousands of native missionaries will go to the lost if Christians in the West will help by sharing resources with them.

This is why I believe God called me to the United States. The only reason I stay here is to help serve our Asian brethren by bringing their needs before God's people in the West. A whole new generation of Christians needs to know that this profound shift in the mission task has taken place. North American believers need to know they still are needed as "senders" to pray and to help the native brothers go.

The waters of missions have been muddied. Today many Christians are unable to think clearly about the real issues because Satan has sent a deceiving spirit to blind their eyes. I don't make this statement lightly. Satan knows that to stop world evangelism he must confuse the minds of Western Christians. This he has done quite effectively. The facts speak for themselves.

The average North American Christian gives only one penny a day to global missions. Imagine what that means. Missions are the primary task of the church, our Lord's final command to us before His ascension. Jesus died on the cross to start a missionary movement. He came to show God's love, and we're left here to continue that mission. Yet this most important task of the church is receiving less than one percent of all our finances.

Of the Western missionaries who are sent overseas, the majority are involved in an unbalanced ministry. Digging wells, operating schools and hospitals, or supporting bands of revolutionary guerrillas is not primarily sharing the gospel. As important as compassionate social concern is in the Third World, it must grow out of the local church. It cannot be superimposed on them by outsiders. The preaching of the gospel will redeem people and produce social change naturally as churches are planted in the villages. The local church is God's tool for Christian caring and sharing.

Approximately 85 percent of all missionary finances are being used by Western missionaries who are working among the established churches on the field — not for pioneer evangelism to the lost. From almost every perspective then, it is obvious that mission spending is being done in areas far from the essence of what real Christian missions is about in the biblical context. The powers of darkness have done a devious job of sidetracking and sabotaging the missionary enterprise of the North American church.

Finally, much of what has passed for missions is really neo-colonial expansionism of our denominations and organizations. In the end, most of that one penny a day the average American Christian has given to missions actually was spent on projects or programs other than proclaiming the whole gospel of Christ. But a shift has taken place in the last forty troubled years.

At the end of World War II, just four short decades ago, almost the entire work of the Great Commission was being done by a handful of white foreigners. To these Christian mission leaders, it was impossible even to imagine reaching all the thousands of distinct cultural groups in the colonies. So they focused their attention on the major cultural groups in easy-to-reach centers of trade and government.

In most of the Asian nations, nearly two hundred years of mission work had been accomplished under the watchful gaze of colonial governors when the era finally ended in 1945. During that time, Western missionaries appeared to be a vital part of the fabric of Western colonial government. Even the few churches that were established among the dominant cultural groups appeared weak. Like the local government and economy, they too were directly controlled by foreigners. Few were indigenous or independent of Western missionaries. Not surprisingly, the masses shunned these strange centers of alien religion, much as most Americans avoid "Krishna missions" in the United States today.

In this atmosphere, the thought of going beyond the major cultural groups — reaching out to the unfinished task — was naturally put off. Those masses of people in rural areas, ethnic subcultures, tribal groups and minorities would have to wait. Teaching them was still generations away — unless, of course, more white foreign missionaries could be recruited to go to them.

But this was not to be. When the colonial-era missionaries returned to take control of "their" churches, hospitals and schools, they found the political climate had changed radically. They met a new hostility from Asian governments. Something radical had happened during World War II. The nationalists had organized and were on the march.

Soon political revolution was sweeping the Third World. And with the independence of one nation after another, the missionaries lost their positions of power and privilege. In the twenty-five years following World War II, seventy-one nations broke free of Western domination. And with their new freedom, most decided Western missionaries would be among the first symbols of the West to go. Now 119 nations — with over half of the world's population — forbid or seriously restrict foreign missionaries.[1]

But there is a bright side to the story. The effect of all this on the emerging churches of Asia has been electric. Far from slowing the spread of the gospel, the gospel began to break free from the Western traditions that had been added to it unwittingly by foreign missionaries.

Sadhu Sunder Singh, a pioneer native missionary evangelist, used to tell a little story that illustrates the importance of presenting the gospel in culturally acceptable terms.

A high caste Hindu, he said, had one day fainted from the summer heat while sitting on a train in a railway station. A train employee ran to a water faucet, filled a cup with water and brought it to the man in an attempt to revive him. But in spite of his condition, the Hindu refused. He would rather die than accept water in the cup of someone from another caste.

Then someone else noticed that the high caste passenger had left his own cup on the seat beside him. So he grabbed it, filled it with water and returned to offer it to the panting victim of the heat. Immediately he accepted the water with gratitude.

Then Sunder Singh would say to his hearers, "This is what I have been trying to say to missionaries from abroad. You have been offering the water of life to the people of India in a foreign cup, and we have been slow to receive it. If you will offer it in our own cup — in an indigenous form — then we are much more likely to accept it."

Today, a whole new generation of Spirit-led young native leaders is mapping strategies to complete the evangelization of our Asian homelands. In almost every country of Asia, I personally know local missionaries who are effectively winning their people to Christ using culturally acceptable methods and styles.

These local missionaries can bridge the cultural gap in their own nations and quite easily go to neighboring countries, taking the gospel for the first time to millions who formerly rejected it as foreign religion.

While there still is persecution in one form or another in most Asian nations, the post-colonial national governments have guaranteed almost unlimited freedom to native missionaries. Just because Westerners have been forbidden, the expansion of the church does not have to cease.

For some diabolical reason, news of this dramatic change has not reached the ears of most believers in our churches. While God by His Holy Spirit has been raising up a new army of missionaries to carry on the work of the Great Commission, most North American believers have sat unmoved. This I have discovered is not because Christians here are lacking in generosity. When they are told the need, they respond quickly. They are not involved only because they don't know the real truth about what is happening in Asia today.

I believe we are being called to be involved by sharing prayerfully and financially in the great work that lies ahead. As we do this, it is possible that together we can see the fulfillment of that awesome prophecy in Revelation 7:9.

> A great number which no man could number, of all nations, and kindreds, and people and tongues, stood before the throne, and before the Lamb, clothed with white robes, and palms in their hands; and cried with a loud voice, saying, "Salvation to our God which sitteth upon the throne, and unto the throne, and unto the Lamb."

This prediction is about to come true. Now, for the first time in history, we can see the final thrust taking place. It is right now happening as God's people everywhere unite to make it possible.

What should intrigue us — especially here in the West — is the way the native missionary movement is flourishing without the help and genius of our Western planning. The Holy Spirit, when we give Him the freedom to work, prompts spontaneous growth and expansion.

Until we can recognize the native missionary movement as the plan of God for this period in history, and until we are willing to become servants to what He is doing, we're in danger of frustrating the will of God.

17

Our Policy Is the Natives

Does what you have read in the previous chapter mean all
Western missionaries should pull out of Asia forever? Of
course not.

God still sovereignly calls Western missionaries to do
unique and special tasks in Asia. But we must understand that
the primary role for Westerners now should be to support
efforts of indigenous mission works through financial aid and
intercessory prayer.

As gently as I can, I have to say anti-American prejudice
still is running high in most of Asia. "There are times in
history," writes Dennis E. Clark in *The Third World and
Mission*, "when however gifted a person may be, he can no
longer effectively proclaim the Gospel to those of another
culture. A German could not have done so in Britain in 1941
nor could an Indian in Pakistan during the war of 1967, and it
will be extremely difficult for Americans to do so in the Third
World of the 1980s and 1990s."[1]

Probably the most difficult message I struggle to proclaim in
North America is that Western missionaries are not welcome in
most nations of Asia. In fact, this is a section I write with the
greatest fear and trembling — but these truths must be said if we
are to accomplish the will of God in the Asian mission fields
today.

153

For the sake of Christ — because the love of Jesus constrains us — we need to review the financial and mission policies of our churches and North American missionary sending agencies. Every believer should reconsider his or her own stewardship practices and submit to the Holy Spirit's guidance in how best to support the global outreach of the church.

I'm not calling for an end to denominational mission programs or the closing down of the many hundreds of missions here in North America — but I am asking us to reconsider the missionary policies and practices that have guided us for the last two hundred years. It is time to make some basic changes and launch the biggest missionary movement in history — one that primarily helps send forth native missionary evangelists rather than a Western staff.

The principle I argue for is this: We believe the most effective way now to win Asia for Christ is through prayer and financial support for the native missionary force that God is raising up in the Third World.

As a general rule, for the following reasons I believe it is wiser to support native missionaries in their own lands than to send Western missionaries.

First, it's bad stewardship to send Western missionaries. At present, the average American missionary family on the field is costing $43,000 a year, and inflation is increasing that cost every day. Based on estimates by C. Peter Wagner, it will cost $163,295 to keep that couple on the field by the year 2000. We're then looking at an annual missionary budget of nearly $117 billion. When you realize that America contributes less than $1 billion now, we're talking about an astronomical fund-raising effort. There has to be an alternative.[2]

During a recent consultation on world evangelism in Thailand, Western missionary leaders called for two hundred thousand new missionaries by the year 2000 in order to keep pace with their estimates of population growth. The cost of even that more modest missionary force is a staggering $4 billion a year.

In India, for only the cost of flying an American from New York to Bombay, a native missionary already on the field can minister for years! Unless we take these facts into account, we will lose the opportunity of our age to reach untold millions with the gospel. Today it is outrageously extravagant to send North American missionaries overseas unless there are compelling reasons to do so. From a strictly financial standpoint, sending American missionaries overseas is one of the worst investments we can make today.

Second, the presence of Western missionaries perpetuates the myth that Christianity is the religion of the West. Roland Allen says it better than I in his classic book *The Spontaneous Expansion of the Church*:

> Even if the supply of men and funds from Western sources was unlimited and we could cover the whole globe with an army of millions of foreign missionaries and establish stations thickly all over the world, the method would speedily reveal its weakness, as it is already beginning to reveal it.
>
> The mere fact that Christianity was propagated by such an army, established in foreign stations all over the world, would inevitably alienate the native populations, who would see in it the growth of the denomination of a foreign people. They would see themselves robbed of their religious independence, and would more and more fear the loss of their social independence.
>
> Foreigners can never successfully direct the propagation of any faith throughout a whole country. If the faith does not become naturalized and expand among the people by its own vital power, it exercises an alarming and hateful influence, and men fear and shun it as something alien. It is then obvious that no sound missionary policy can be based upon multiplication of missionaries and mis-

sion stations. A thousand would not suffice; a dozen might be too many.[3]

A friend of mine who heads a missionary organization similar to ours recently told me the story of a conversation he had with some African church leaders.

"We want to evangelize our people," they said, "but we can't do it so long as the white missionaries remain. Our people won't listen to us. The communists and the Moslems tell them all white missionaries are spies sent out by their governments as agents for the capitalistic imperialists. We know it isn't true, but newspaper reports tell of how some missionaries are getting funds from the CIA. We love the American missionaries in the Lord. We wish they could stay, but the only hope for us to evangelize our own country is for all white missionaries to leave."

Untold millions still are being wasted today by our denominations and missions as they erect and protect elaborate organizational frameworks overseas. There was a time when Western missionaries needed to go into these countries where the gospel was not preached. But now a new era has begun, and it is important that we officially acknowledge this. God has raised up indigenous leaders in every nation who are more capable than outsiders to finish the job.

Now we must send the major portion of our funds to native missionaries and church growth movements. But this doesn't mean we don't appreciate the legacy left to us from Western missionaries. While I believe changes must be made in our missionary methods, we praise God for the tremendous contribution Western missionaries have made in many Third World countries where Christ never was preached before. Through their faithfulness many were won to Jesus, churches were started and the Scriptures were translated. And it is these converts who now are today's native missionaries.

Silas Fox, a Canadian who served in South India, learned to speak the local native language Telegu and preached the Word with such anointing that hundreds of present-day Christian leaders in Andhra Pradesh can trace their spiritual beginnings to his ministry.

I thank God for missionaries like Hudson Taylor, who against all wishes of his foreign mission board became a Chinese in his life-style and won many to Christ. I am not worthy to wipe the dust from the feet of thousands of faithful men and women of our Lord who went overseas during the times of men and women like these.

Jesus set the example. "As my Father hath sent me," He said, "even so send I you" (John 20:21). The Lord became one of us in order to win us to the love of God. He knew He couldn't be an alien from outer space so He became incarnated into our bodies.

For any missionary to be successful he must identify with the people he plans to reach. Because Westerners usually can't do this, they are ineffective. Anyone — Asian or American — who insists on still going out as a representative of Western missions and organizations will be ineffective today. We cannot maintain a Western life-style or outlook and work among the poor of Asia.

Third, with the Western missionaries and the money they bring, the natural growth and independence of the national church is compromised. The economic power of the North American dollar distorts the picture as North American missionaries hire key national leaders to run their organizations.

Recently I met with a missionary executive of one of the major U.S. denominations. He is a loving man whom I deeply respect as a brother in Christ, but he heads the colonial-style extension of his denomination into Asia.

We talked about mutual friends and the exciting growth that is occurring in the national churches of India. We shared much in the Lord. I quickly found he had as much respect as I did for the Indian brothers God is choosing to use in India today. Yet he wouldn't support these men who are so obviously anointed by God.

I asked him why. (His denomination is spending millions of

dollars annually to open up their brand of churches in Asia — money I felt could be far better used supporting native missionaries in the churches the Holy Spirit is spontaneously birthing.)

His answer shocked and saddened me.

"Our policy," he admitted without shame, "is to use the nationals only to expand churches with our denominational distinctives."

The words rolled around in my mind, "use the nationals." This is what colonialism was all about, and it is still what neo-colonialism of most Western missions is all about. With their money and technology, many organizations are simply buying people to perpetuate their foreign denominations, ways and beliefs.

In Thailand a group of native missionaries was "bought away" by a powerful American parachurch organization. Once effectively winning their own people to Christ and planting churches in the Thai way, their leaders were given scholarships to train in the United States. The American organization provided them with expense accounts, vehicles and posh offices in Bangkok.

What price did the native missionary leader pay? He must use foreign literature, films and the standard method of this highly technical American organization. No consideration is being made of how effective these tools and methods will be in building the Thai church. They will be used whether they are effective or not because they are written into the training manuals and handbooks of this organization.

After all, the reasoning of this group goes, these programs worked in Los Angeles and Dallas — they must work in Thailand as well!

This kind of thinking is the worst neo-colonialism. To use God-given money to hire people to perpetuate our ways and theories is a modern method of old-fashioned imperialism. No method could be more unbiblical.

The sad fact is this. God already was doing a wonderful work in Thailand by His Holy Spirit in a culturally acceptable way. Why didn't this American group have the humility to bow before the

Holy Spirit and say, "Have Thine own way, Lord." If they wanted to help, I think the best way would have been to support what God already was doing by His Holy Spirit. By the time this group finds out what a mistake it has made, the missionaries who messed up the local church will be going home for furlough — probably never to return.

At their rallies they will tell stories of victories in Thailand as they evangelized the country American-style; but no one will be asking the most important question, Where is the fruit that remains?

Often we become so preoccupied with expanding our own organizations that we do not comprehend the great sweep of the Holy Spirit of God as He has moved upon the peoples of the world. Intent upon building "our" churches, we have failed to see how Christ is building "His" church in every nation. We must stop looking at the lost world through the eyes of our particular denomination. Then we will be able to win the lost souls to Jesus instead of trying to add more numbers to our man-made organizations to please the headquarters that control the funds.

Fourth, Western missionaries cannot go to the countries where most so-called hidden people live. About 2.7 billion of these people exist in our world today. There are the millions upon millions of lost souls who have never heard the gospel. We hear many cries that we should go to them. But who will go? These people are almost all living in countries closed or severely restricted to American and European missionaries. Although half the countries in the world today forbid the Western missionary, now the native missionary can go to the nearest hidden people group. For example, an Indian can go to Nepal with the gospel; North Americans can't.

Of the more than seventy thousand North American missionaries now actively commissioned, only five thousand are working with the totally unreached hidden people who make up 70 percent of all the unevangelized people in the world. Ralph Winter, general director of the U.S. Center for World Mission, estimates 95 percent of all missionaries are working among the existing churches or where the gospel already is preached.

Fifth, Western missionaries seldom are effective. Unlike the Western missionary, the native missionary can preach, teach and evangelize without being blocked by most of the barriers that confront Westerners. As a native of the country or region, he knows the cultural taboos instinctively. Frequently, he already has mastered the language or a related dialect. He moves freely and is accepted in good times and bad as one who belongs.

He does not have to be transported thousands of miles nor does he require special training and language schools.

The truth of the matter is this: *Western missionaries seldom are effective today in reaching Asians and establishing local churches in the villages of Asia.*

I remember an incident — one of many — that illustrates this sad fact.

During my days of preaching in the northwest of India, I met a missionary from New Zealand involved in Christian literature ministry. She had been a missionary in India for twenty-five years; and during her final term, she was assigned to a Christian bookstore. One day as my team and I went to her shop to buy some books, we found the book shop closed. When we went to her missionary quarters — which was in a walled mansion — we asked what was happening. She replied, "I am going back home for good."

I asked what would happen to the ministry of the book shop. She answered, "I have sold all the books at wholesale price, and I have closed down everything."

With deep hurt, I asked her if there wasn't anyone she could have handed the store over to in order to continue the work.

"No, I could not find anyone," she replied. And I wondered why, after twenty-five years of being in India, she was leaving without one person whom she had won to Christ, no disciple to continue her work. She, along with her missionary colleagues, lived in walled compounds with three or four servants each to look after their life-style. She spent a lifetime and untold amounts of God's precious money which could have been used to preach the gospel. I could not help but think Jesus had called us to become servants — not masters. Had she done so, she would have fulfilled the call of God upon her life and fulfilled the Great Commission.

Unfortunately, this is a sad truth that is being repeated all over the world of colonial-style foreign missions. Regrettably, seldom are Western missionaries being held accountable for the current lack of results, nor is their failure being reported at home in the United States and Canada.

But at the same time, native evangelists are seeing thousands turn to Christ in revival movements on every continent. Hundreds of new churches are being formed every week by native missionaries in the Third World!

Not a Mission but a
Theological Problem

God obviously is moving mightily among native believers. These are the wonderful, final days of Christian history. Now is the time for the whole family of God to unite and share with one another, as the New Testament church did, the richer churches giving to the poorer.

The body of Christ in the East is looking to the West to link hands with them in this time of harvest and to support the work with the material blessings that God has showered upon them. With the love and support of North American believers, we can help native evangelists and their families march forward and complete the task of world evangelization in this century.

As I sit on platforms and stand in pulpits all across North America, I am speaking on behalf of the native brethren. God has called me to be the servant of the needy brothers who cannot speak up for themselves in North America.

As I wait to speak, I look out over the congregation, and I often pray for some of the missionaries by name. Usually I pray something like this: "Lord Jesus, I am about to stand here on behalf of Thomas John and P.T. Steven tonight. May I represent them faithfully. Help us to meet their needs through this meeting."

Of course, the names of the native missionaries change each

time. But I believe the will of God will not be accomplished in our generation unless this audience and many others like it respond to the cry of the lost. Each of us must follow the Lord in the place to which He has called us — the native evangelist in his land and the sponsors here in this land. Some obey by going; others obey by supporting. Even if you cannot go to Asia, you can fulfill the Great Commission by helping send native brothers to the pioneer fields.

This — and many other similar truths about missions — are no longer understood in the West. Preaching and teaching about missions has been lost in most of our churches. The sad result is seen everywhere. Most believers no longer can define what a missionary is, what he or she does, or what the work of the church is as it relates to the Great Commission.

A declining interest in missions is the sure sign that a church and people have left their first love. Nothing is more indicative of the moral decline of the West than Christians who have lost the passion of Christ for a lost and dying world.

The older I become, the more I understand the real reason millions go to hell without hearing the gospel.

Actually, this is not a mission problem. It is a theological problem — a problem of misunderstanding and unbelief. Many churches have slipped so far from biblical teaching that Christians cannot explain why the Lord left us here on earth.

All of us are called for a purpose. Some years ago when I was in North India, a little boy about eight years old watched me as I prepared for my morning meditations. I began to talk to him about Jesus and asked him several questions.

"What are you doing?" I asked the lad.

"I go to school" was the reply.

"Why do you go to school?"

"To study," he said.

"Why do you study?"

"To get smart."

"Why do you want to get smart?"

"So I can get a good job."

"Why do you want to get a good job?"

"So I can make lots of money."

"Why do you want to make lots of money?"

"So I can buy food."

"Why do you want to buy food?"

"So I can eat."

"Why do you want to eat?"

"To live."

"Why do you live?"

At that point, the little boy thought for a minute, scratched his head, looked me in the face and said, "Sir, why do I live?" He paused a moment in mid-thought, then gave his own sad answer, "To die!"

The question is the same for all of us: Why do we live?

What is the basic purpose of your living in this world, as you claim to be a disciple of the Lord Jesus Christ?

Is it to accumulate wealth? Fame? Popularity? To fulfill the desires of the flesh and of the mind? And to somehow survive and, in the end, to die and hopefully go to heaven?

No. The purpose of your life as a believer must be to obey Jesus when He said, "Go ye into all the world and preach the gospel...."

That is what Paul did when he laid down his arms and said, "Lord, what do You want me to do?"

If all of your concern is about your own life, your job, your clothes, your children's good clothes, healthy bodies, a good education, a good job and marriage, then your concerns are no different from a heathen's in Bhutan, Burma or India.

In recent months I have looked back on those seven years of village evangelism as one of the greatest learning experiences of my life. We walked in Jesus' steps, incarnating and representing Him to masses of people who had never heard the gospel.

When Jesus was here on earth, His goal was to do nothing but the will of His Father. Our commitment must be only His will.

Jesus no longer is walking on earth. We are His body; He is our head. That means our lips are the lips of Jesus. Our hands are His hands; our eyes, His eyes; our hope, His hope.

My wife and children belong to Jesus. My money, my talent, my education — all belong to Jesus.

So what is His will? What are we to do in this world with all of these gifts He has given us?

"As the Father has sent Me, even so send I you" are His instructions. "Go into all the world and make disciples, teaching them to obey all these things, and lo, I am with you even until the end of the age."

Every Christian should know the answers to some basic questions about missions in order to fulfill the call of our Lord to reach the lost world for His name.

First, what is the primary task of the church? Each of the four Gospels — Matthew, Mark, Luke and John — gives us a war cry from our Lord Jesus. This challenge from Christ is the mission statement of the church. Through the years it has become known as the Great Commission and it summarizes the main activity of the church until Jesus returns as King of kings to gather us to Himself.

Essentially it reveals the reason God has left us here in this world. He desires us to be mobilized to go everywhere proclaiming the love of God to a lost world. Exercising His authority and demonstrating His power, we are to preach the gospel, make disciples, baptize and teach people to obey all the commands of Christ.

So this task is a lot more than handing out leaflets, holding street meetings or showing compassionate love to the sick and hungry. These are all involved, of course. But the Lord is expecting much more of us. He wants us to continue as His agents to redeem and transform the lives of people. Disciple-making, as Jesus defined it, obviously involves the long-time process of planting local churches.

And all these references to the Great Commission are accompanied by promises of divine power: Matthew 28:18-20; Mark 16:15-18; Luke 24:47-49; Acts 1:8. The global expansion of the church obviously is a task for a special people who are living intimately enough with God to discern and exercise His authority.

Which brings us to the second question.

Who is a missionary? A missionary is anyone sent out by the Lord to establish a new Christian witness where such a witness still is unknown. As we traditionally define it today, it usually involves leaving our own immediate culture for another. For example, we usually define a missionary as anyone who takes the gospel to people who differ in at least one aspect — such as language, nationality, race or tribe — from his or her own ethnic group.

For some strange reason, many North Americans have come to believe that a missionary is only someone from the West who goes to Asia, Africa or some other foreign land. Not so. When a former Hindu Brahmin crosses the subtle caste lines of India and works among low-caste people, he should be recognized as a missionary just as much as a person who goes from Detroit to Calcutta.

Christians in the West must abandon the totally unscriptural idea that they should support only white missionaries from America. Today it is essential that we support missionaries going from South India to North India, from one island of the Philippines to another, or from Korea to China.

Unless we abandon the racism implied in our unwritten definition of a missionary, we never will see the world reached for Christ. While governments may close the borders of their countries to Western missionaries, they cannot close them to their own people. The Lord is raising up such an army of national missionaries right now, but they cannot go unless North Americans will continue to support the work as they did when white Westerners were allowed.

Finally, where is the mission field? One of the biggest mistakes we make is to define mission fields in terms of nation states. These are only political boundaries established along arbitrary lines through wars or by natural boundaries such as mountain ranges and rivers.

A more biblical definition conforms to the linguistic and tribal groupings. So a mission field is defined as any cultural group which does not have an established group of disciples.

For example, the Arabs of New York City or the people of the Hopi Indian tribe in Dallas are unreached people groups in the United States. There are over sixteen thousand such hidden people groups worldwide — and they represent the real pioneer mission fields of our time.

They will be reached only if someone from *outside* their culture is willing to sacrifice his or her own comfortable community to reach them with the gospel of Christ. And to go and do so, that person needs some believers at home who will stand behind him with prayers and finances.

The native missionary movement in Asia — because it is close at hand to most of the world's unreached peoples — can most easily send the evangelists. But they cannot always raise the needed support among their destitute populations. This is where Christians in the West can come forward, sharing their abundance with God's servants in Asia.

Missionary statesman George Verwer believes most North American Christians are still only playing soldiers. But just as he does, I know here and there across America there are individuals and groups who believe that, at any cost, the sleeping giant in our nation should be aroused. We are capable of supporting the needed missionaries and we should not rest until the task is complete.

You may never be called personally to reach the hidden peoples of Asia; but through soldier-like suffering at home you can make it possible for millions to hear overseas.

Today I'm calling on Christians to give up their stale Christianity to use the weapons of spiritual warfare and to advance against the enemy. We must stop skipping over the verses which read, "If anyone would come after me, he must deny himself and take up his cross and follow me" and "Any of you who does not give up everything he has cannot be my disciple" (Matt. 16:24; Luke 14:33, NIV).

Were these verses written only for the native missionaries who are on the front lines being stoned and beaten and going hungry for their faith? Or were they written only for North American believers comfortably going through the motions of church, teaching conferences and concerts?

Of course not. These verses apply equally to Christians in Bangkok, Boston and Bombay.

Says Verwer, "Some missionary magazines and books leave one with the impression that worldwide evangelization is only a matter of time. More careful research will show that in densely populated areas the work of evangelism is going backward rather than forward.

"In view of this, our tactics are simply crazy. Perhaps 80 percent of our efforts for Christ — weak as they often are — still are aimed at only 20 percent of the world's population. Literally hundreds of millions of dollars are poured into every kind of Christian project at home, especially buildings, while only a thin trickle goes out to the regions beyond. Half-hearted saints believe by giving just a few hundred dollars they have done their share. We all have measured ourselves so long by the man next to us we barely can see the standard set by men like Paul or by Jesus Himself.

"During the Second World War, the British showed themselves capable of astonishing sacrifices (as did many other nations). They lived on meager, poor rations. They cut down their railings and sent them for weapons manufacture. Yet today, in what is more truly a (spiritual) World War, Christians live as peacetime soldiers. Look at Paul's injunctions to Timothy in 2 Timothy 2:3-4: 'Endure hardship with us like a good soldier of Christ Jesus.

No one serving as a soldier gets involved with civilian affairs — he wants to please his commanding officer.' We seem to have a strange idea of Christian service. We will buy books, travel miles to hear a speaker on blessings, pay large sums to listen to a group singing the latest Christian songs — but we forget that we are soldiers."1

Day after day I continue with this one message: Hungry, hurting, native missionaries are waiting to go on to the next village with the gospel, but they need your prayer and financial support. We're facing a new day in missions, but it requires the cooperation of Christians in both the East and West.

19

Lord, Help Us
Remain True to You

Yes, today God is working in a miraculous way. Without all the trappings of high-powered promotion, an increasing number of believers are catching the vision of God's third wave in missions. We already have seen thousands of individuals raised up to share in the work. But I believe this is also only a foretaste of the millions more who will respond in the days ahead. Many pastors, church leaders, former missionaries, and Christian broadcasters in North America are also unselfishly lending their support.

In addition to these sponsors and donors, volunteers are organizing local prayer bands and coordinating united efforts at the grass-roots level throughout Canada and the United States. Without this network of local workers to help provide the needed support, there is no human way the missionary task of the church will be completed. Local GFA coordinators, who work without payment, help represent the work of Gospel for Asia by distributing *SEND* newspapers free through Christian bookstores, churches, women's groups and prayer meetings.

They are also helping organize home meetings, speaking at churches or small groups, and explaining the sponsorship program. They do whatever else is necessary to minister and share the message in the supporting nations.

These sponsors, like the poor widow Jesus commended for giving all she had, make great sacrifices.

I'll never forget one dear retired widow whom I met on a speaking tour. Excited about how much she still could do even though she wasn't working, she pledged to sponsor a missionary out of her tiny Social Security check.

After six months I received a very sad letter from her. "Brother K.P.," she wrote, "I am so privileged to be supporting a missionary. I'm living all alone now on only a fixed income. I know when I get to heaven I'm going to meet people who have come to Christ through my sharing, but I must reduce my support because my utility bills have gone up. Please pray for me that I will find a way to give my full support again."

When my wife, Gisela, showed me the letter, I was deeply touched. I called the woman and told her she need not feel guilty — she was doing all she could. I even advised her not to give if it became a greater hardship.

Two weeks later, another letter came. "Every day," she wrote, "I've been praying for a way to find some more money for my missionary. As I prayed, the Lord showed me a way — I've disconnected my phone."

I looked at the check. Tears came to my eyes as I thought how much this woman was sacrificing. She must be lonely, I thought. What would happen if she got sick? Without a phone, she would be cut off from the world. "Lord," I prayed, as I held the check in both hands, "help us to remain true to You and honor this great sacrifice." Another gift, this time from a thirteen-year-old boy named Tommy, shows the same spirit of sacrifice.

For over a year Tommy had been saving for a new bicycle for school. Then he read about the value of bicycles to native missionaries like Mohan Ram and his wife from Tamil Nadu State. Since 1977, Ram had been walking in the scorching sun between villages. He and his wife were engaged in church planting. With his family, he lived in one rented room and had to walk for miles or ride buses to do gospel work.

His outreach (Bible classes, open-air evangelism, tract distribution, children's classes and Bible translation) was directly dependent on his ability to travel. A bicycle would mean more to him than a car would mean to someone in suburban America.

But a new Indian-made bicycle, which would cost only ninety-two dollars, was totally out of reach of his family budget. What amazed me when I came to America is that bikes here are considered children's toys or a way to lose weight. For native missionaries they represent a way to expand the ministry greatly and reduce suffering.

When Tommy heard that native missionaries use their bikes to ride seventeen to twenty miles a day, he made a big decision. He decided to give to GFA the bike money he had saved.

"I can use my brother's old bike," he wrote. "My dad has given me permission to send you my new bike money for the native missionary."

Another teenager, seventeen-year-old Todd, sponsored five missionaries a month. To accomplish this task, he worked two part-time jobs and gave up ice cream and other treats. Not satisfied, he organized a walk-a-thon among friends and sent us twelve hundred dollars more.

A tireless volunteer, he actively distributed *SEND* in local churches and Christian organizations. Seeking to enlist others as sponsors, he wrote twenty-five letters by hand to friends. We received a check for six hundred dollars from such activity.

Seeing his zeal, we expected to meet an extreme extrovert. But instead, he was shy and quiet — someone who made an intelligent decision to set goals rather than accumulate wealth.

Several times we have received large gifts — as much as twenty thousand dollars and thirty thousand dollars at one time — with unusual explanations attached.

One couple wrote, "We have prayed, and we don't want to leave our money to the world. We want to give everything for eternity. The way we can do this is *not to leave it to our kids*. Here is what we had laid aside for them."

Another woman wrote a similar letter: "The Lord has for some time been speaking to me about money I've been saving up for a rainy day. I want to give it now while I can. Please use it for the native brethren."

Sometimes people find unusual ways to raise extra support. One factory worker goes through all the trash cans at his workplace collecting aluminum beverage cans. Each month we get a check from him — usually enough to sponsor two or more missionaries.

Many churches and pastors also have started to include native evangelists in their mission budgets.

One pastor, Skip Heitzig of the Calvary Chapel in Albuquerque, New Mexico, now supports several missionaries. Like other pastors, he has been sent overseas by his congregation to learn about the native work there. Through Skip's influence, a number of other pastors also have started to include GFA in their regular mission budgets.

In addition to his congregation's ever-increasing monthly support, he has had GFA staff make several presentations at the church. As a result, two dozen individual families in the church also have taken on a family sponsorship.

Churches in nearly every state of the United States now include GFA in their regular mission budgets. One church in Florida sends more than a thousand dollars a month. Another in Plano, Texas, gives 5 percent of the church's gross income to the native missionary movement. (That church, a non-denominational congregation, made their decision after telephone calls to several sources to check on the validity of our work. I had never met the pastor.)

When a congregation in Kelso, Tennessee, made a decision to disband and merge with another church, they sold their property and sent the total proceeds to GFA — one of the largest single donations we've ever received.

Missionaries and former missionaries are among some of our most ardent supporters.

Nina Drew, a retired missionary who spent thirty years in India as a medical volunteer, is so excited about the native missionary movement she says she never would go back to India as a missionary again.

"I believe in this work," she told me. "You are getting more results than we ever did in all our years. I wouldn't return on the same basis again.... Native missionaries are the only way. I think God raised us up as an interim thing only. What is happening now is the permanent reality."

Miss Drew, who came to work among Muslims in a difficult area of North India, was a nurse and certified midwife. In her thirty years of work in India, she saw only one family converted. And she says now they are not living openly for the Lord.

"Sometimes I wonder if it was worth it," she admits.

When Miss Drew came to India in 1945, the British empire already was disintegrating, and she was an eyewitness to the terror and bloodshed of partition — when India and Pakistan were separated from each other in bloody, religious warfare.

Now she works in her native New Zealand, raising money for the native missionary movement in India.

"I feel my ministry at home today is much more productive than most of the work I did while in India," she declared.

Miss Drew said the native missionary movement is the biggest change in modern India.

"This is tremendous!" she exclaimed. "God is raising up hundreds of native brethren in our places."

When asked what strategy she believes the Western church should follow to evangelize India, Miss Drew has only one message:

"Tell God's people in America to support the native workers. It is the only way...the only way."

Another young woman, whose missionary parents have served in India for thirty years, said, "I always wondered why my parents didn't see people coming to Jesus in their work. Now I'm glad I can sponsor a native missionary who is fruitful."

Another "missionary kid" wrote, "My parents were missionaries in Maharashtra for thirty-seven years. I had the opportunity of living the first sixteen of my life there.

"I know something of the difficulty of witnessing for Christ in that dark land. Having looked at your criteria for native missionaries and realizing the many advantages they have over Western missionaries — as well as the fact that the doors are still open to them — I am enclosing a check for the first year of support of a new missionary in India. This will, prayerfully, be a long-time commitment to the continued evangelization of that great land."

Some of the most interesting support for the work has come from other Christian organizations in the United States. Some have loaned us mailing lists or allowed us to participate in their programs and special events.

For example, we were invited to participate in the Keith Green Memorial Concert Tour as the official representative of Third World missions. Melody Green, the widow of recording artist Keith Green, has personally sponsored two native missionaries.

One of the dearest friends of the work has been David Mains of Chapel of the Air in Wheaton, Illinois. Through my guest visits on the Chapel broadcast, sponsors have joined our family from all over the United States. David and Karen have advised and helped us in a number of much-needed areas — including the publishing of this book.

While David and Karen never have said anything about sacrificial giving, I know they have helped us during periods when their own ministry was experiencing financial stress. But Scripture is true when it says, "Give, and it shall be given unto you" (Luke 6:38). One of the unchanging laws of the kingdom is that we must always be giving away from ourselves — both in good times and bad.

How many North American churches, Christian ministries and individuals are experiencing financial difficulties because they have disobeyed these clear commands of God to share?

I could list many others who have helped, but one more whom I must mention is Bob Walker, the long-time publisher and editor of *Christian Life* magazine. Sensitive to the Holy Spirit, Bob was willing to give us a chance to tell our story when many others took a wait-and-see attitude toward our new ministry.

Although we were completely unknown in the early days, Bob didn't turn me away as other publishers did. He prayed about us and said he felt led of God to run articles and reports on the work. Bob also shared his mailing list with us, endorsing our ministry and urging his readers to support the native missionary movement.

It is this kind of open-handed sharing that helped launch the work in the beginning and keeps us growing now. In our weekly nights of prayer and in regular prayer meetings, we constantly remember to thank God for these kinds of favors — and pray that more leaders will be touched with the need of sharing their resources with the Third World.

Perhaps the most exciting long-range development has been a slow but steady shift in the attitude of North American mission agencies and denominations toward native mission movements.

One after another, older missions and denominations have changed anti-native policies and are beginning to support native missionary movements as equal partners in the work of the gospel. The old racism and colonial mind-set are slowly but surely disappearing.

This, I believe, could have long-range impact. If North American denominations and older mission societies would use their massive networks of support to raise funding for native missions, it would be possible for us and similar native missionary ministries to support several hundred thousand more native missionaries in the Third World.

Asks John Haggai, "In a day when an estimated three-fourths of the Third World's people live in countries that either discourage or flatly prohibit foreign missionary efforts, what other way is there to obey Jesus Christ's directive to evangelize all the world?

"For many thoughtful Christians the answer is becoming more and more clear: In those closed countries, evangelization through trained national Christian leaders is the logical way.... Some observers have gone so far as to say it may be the only way."

Haggai's viewpoints are becoming more and more common, and a shifting of opinion and strategy is taking place that I believe will change the complexion of missions almost completely by the end of this decade.

The day of the native missionary movement has come. The seeds have been planted. Ahead of us lie much cultivation and nurture, but it can happen if we will share our resources as the apostle Paul outlined in 2 Corinthians 8 and 9.

There Paul urges the wealthy Christians to collect monies and send support to the poor churches in order that "equality may abound" in the whole body of Christ. Those who have are obligated to share with those who have not, he argues, because of Christ's example.

"For you know the grace of our Lord Jesus Christ, that though he was rich, yet for your sakes he became poor, so that you through his poverty might become rich" (2 Cor. 8:9).

This is the New Testament cry I'm repeating to the wealthy and affluent Christians of the West. Many are becoming more willing to follow the example of our Lord Jesus. He made Himself poor for the salvation of others.

How many are ready to live for eternity and follow His example into a more sacrificial life-style? How many will join in the spirit of suffering of the native brethren?

They are hungry, naked and homeless for the sake of Christ.

I'm not asking North Americans to join them — sleeping along roadsides and going to prison for their witness. But I am asking believers to share in the most practical ways possible — through financial sharing and intercessory prayer.

Here is the true story of a couple who has demonstrated real spiritual understanding. Recently they wrote, "While reading your *SEND* publication, the Lord began to speak to us about going to India. As we pondered this and asked the Lord about it, He spoke again and said, 'You're not going physically, but you're going spiritually and financially.'

"Well, praise the Lord — here is our 'first trip' to India. Please use this money where you see the greatest need. May God's richest blessing be upon you and your ministry."

Enclosed was a check for one thousand dollars. It was signed, "Fellow workers in Christ, Jim and Betty."

My prayer? For several hundred thousand more like Jim and Betty. This dedicated couple has what it takes: the spiritual sensitivity to hear what the Lord is really saying today to the North American church.

20

We Are Walking
in the Narrow Way

He smiled warmly at me from across his big polished desk. I was very impressed. This man led one of the greatest ministries in America. I had admired his ministry for years. He was a great preacher, author and leader. I knew he had a huge following, both among clergy and lay people. (To protect his identity in these pages, I'm going to change some details in the story and not give his name. This incident took place in the very early days of our ministry.)

I was flattered that he had sent me a plane ticket and had invited me to fly across the country to advise him on expanding his work in India. His interest in GFA and the native missionary movement pleased me much more than I was willing to let him believe. From the minute he had first called me, I sensed that here was a man who could be a valuable friend to us in many ways. Perhaps he would open the doors and help us provide sponsorships for some of the hundreds of native missionaries waiting for our support.

But I really wasn't ready for the generous offer he made — one which would turn out to be the first of many tests for me and our mission.

"Brother K.P.," he said slowly, "would you consider giving up what you're doing here in the United States and go back to India as our special representative? We believe that God is calling you to work with us — take the message of our church back to the people of India. We'll back you up 100 percent to do it.

"Whatever you need," he went on without pausing for breath. "We'll give you a printing press and vans and literature. We're prepared to provide you with all the funding, many times what you can raise yourself."

It was an exciting offer. He made it sound even sweeter while I listened. "You can give up all this traveling and raising money. You won't need an office and staff in the States. We'll do all that for you. You want to be in Asia, don't you? That's where the work is — so we'll free you to go back and run the work there."

Weakened by the thought of having so many of my prayers answered in one stroke, I let my mind play with the possibilities. This could be the biggest answer to prayer we've ever had, I thought. As we talked, my eyes unconsciously wandered across the desk to an album of his best-selling teaching tapes. They were well-done, a series on some controversial issues that were sweeping across the States at that time. However, it was irrelevant to our needs and problems in Asia.

But seeing what appeared to be my interest in the cassettes, he spoke with a sudden burst of self-assurance. "We'll start with these tapes," he said as he handed them to me. "I'll give you the support you need to produce them in India. We can even have them translated in all the major languages. We'll produce millions of copies and get this message into the hands of every Indian believer." I'd heard other men with the same wild idea. The tapes would be useless in India. Millions were going to hell in India. They didn't need this man's message at all. Although I thought his idea was insane, I tried to be polite.

"Well," I offered lamely, "there might be some material here that could be adapted for India and printed as a booklet."

Suddenly his face froze. I sensed that I had said something wrong. "Oh, no," he said with an air of stubborn finality, "I can't change a word. That's the message God gave me. It's part of what we're all about. If it's not a problem in India now, it soon will be. We need you to help us get the word out all over Asia."

In an instant this basically good man of God had shown his real colors. His heart wasn't really burning with a passion for the lost at all — or for the churches of Asia. This man had an axe to grind, and he thought he had the money to hire me to grind it for him overseas. It was the same old story — a case of religious neo-colonialism.

So here I was, face-to-face again with pride and flesh in all its ugliness. I admired and liked this man and his ministry, but he had only one problem. He believed, as many before him have, that if God was doing anything in the world, He would do it through him.

As soon as I could, I excused myself politely and never called him back. He was living in a world of the past, in the day of colonial missions when Western denominations could export and peddle their doctrines and programs to the emerging churches of Asia.

The body of Christ in Asia owes a great debt to the wonderful missionaries who came in the nineteenth and twentieth centuries. They brought the gospel to us and planted the church. But the church now needs to be released from Western domination.

My message to the West is simple: God is calling Christians everywhere to recognize that He is building His church in Asia. Your support is needed for the native missionaries whom God is raising up to extend His church — but not to impose your man-made controls and teachings on the Eastern churches.

And we've faced other tests. The biggest perhaps came from another group that also shall remain unidentified. This time it involved the biggest single gift ever offered us.

Our friendship and love for these men have developed over the last few years. We have seen God birth into their hearts a burden to see the gospel of the Lord Jesus preached in the demonstration of the power of God throughout the world. God has given them a desire to be involved in the equipping of these native pastors and evangelists, and they have helped GFA financially with projects over the last several years.

Once, by apparent chance, I accidentally ran into a delegation of four of their American brothers in India. After meeting some of our native missionaries, I could see that the visitors were significantly challenged by the lives of the Indian evangelists.

Privately, they exclaimed how deeply touched they were by the effectiveness of the native workers and with the work God was doing through them. When I returned home, letters of thanks were waiting for me, and a couple of the men offered to sponsor a native missionary. This gesture was amazing to me because these same men also were voting to give us financial grants for other projects. It convinced me they really believed in the work of the native brethren — enough to get personally involved beyond their official duties as trustees.

Imagine the way I shouted and danced around the office when I got another call from the chairman of this board two weeks later.

They had decided, he said, to give us a huge amount from their missionary budget! It was beyond my comprehension even to imagine a gift that size. When I hung up the phone, the staff in our office thought I'd gone crazy. How desperately we needed that money. In fact, in my mind I already had it spent. The first part would go, I thought, to start the intensive missionary training institute for new missionaries.

And that's why, perhaps, the next development was such a blow. As members of their board discussed the project among themselves, questions arose about accountability and control. They phoned me. The leaders expressed that probably the only way the board would agree to support the project would be for a representative of their organization to be on the board of the institute in India. After all, that large amount of money just could not be released with "no strings attached."

The request went through my heart like a knife. This was a real surprise. I couldn't do that. Through all the years, I always personally had refused to sit on any of the native mission boards we support in Asia. To suggest an outsider sit on the board of this new indigenous work would betray my brethren and take them back into bondage of men. We always have given our aid without demanding control of an indigenous ministry.

Taking a deep breath and asking the Lord for help, I tried to explain why we don't sit on native boards and why I couldn't accept a gift that required one of their directors to sit on the indigenous board.

"Our leaders overseas fast and pray about every decision," I said. "We don't have to sit on their boards to protect our monies. It's not our money, anyway; it belongs to God. He is greater than GFA or your organization. Let God protect His own interests. The native brethren don't need you or me to be their leader. Jesus is their Lord, and He will lead them in the right way to use the grant."

The silence on the other end of the line was long.

"I'm sorry, Brother K.P.," said the director finally. "I don't think I can sell this idea to our board of directors. They want accountability for the money. How can they have that without putting a man on the board? Be reasonable. You're making it very hard on us to help. This is standard policy for a gift this size."

My mind raced. A little voice said, "Go ahead. All they want is a worthless piece of paper. Don't make an issue of this. After all, this is the biggest grant you've ever received. Nobody gives big money away like this without some control. Stop being a fool."

But I knew I could not consent to that proposal. I couldn't face the Asian brethren and say that in order to get this money, they had to have an American fly halfway around the world to approve how they spent it. "No," I said, "we cannot accept your money if it means compromising the purity of our ministry. We have plenty of accountability through the trusted godly men who have been appointed to the native board. Later, you can see the building yourself when you go to Asia. I can't compromise the autonomy of the work by putting an American on the native board.

"What you are suggesting is that you want to 'steady the ark' as Uzzah did in the Old Testament. God slew him because he presumed to control the working of God. When the Holy Spirit moves and does His work, we become restless because we want to control it. It is an inherent weakness of the flesh. The bottom line of your offer is to control the work in Asia with hidden strings attached to your gift. You have to learn to let your money go, because it is not your money but God's."

Then, with my heart in my mouth, I gave him one last argument, hoping it could save the gift — but willing to lose all if I was unable to convince them.

"Brother," I said quietly, "I sign checks for hundreds of thousands of dollars and send them to the field every month. Many times as I hold those big checks in my hand, I pray, 'Lord, this is Your money. I'm just a steward sending it where You said it should go. Help the leaders on the field use this money to win the lost millions and glorify the name of Jesus.'

"All we must be concerned about is doing our part. I obey the Holy Spirit in dispensing the Lord's money. Don't ask me to ask the native brethren to do something I won't do."

I paused. What more could I say?

"Well," the voice at the other end of the line repeated, "we really want to help. I will make the presentation, but you're making it very hard for me."

"I'm sure," I said with conviction, "there are other organizations that will meet your requirement. I just know we can't. Fellowship in the gospel is one thing — but outside control is unbiblical and in the end harms the work more than helping it."

I said it with conviction, but inside I was sure we had lost the grant. There was nothing more to say, so we both said good-bye. I waited for some word. Two weeks passed without a contact. Every day I prayed God would help the whole board of directors understand. Our inner circle — people who knew about the expected gift — kept asking me if I'd heard anything. Our whole office was praying.

"We're walking in the narrow way," I said bravely to the staff, "doing what God has told us." Inside I kept wishing God would let me bend the rules a little this time.

But our faithfulness paid off. One day the phone rang, and it was the director again. The board had met the night before, and he had presented my position to them.

"Brother K.P.," he said with a smile in his voice, "we have met and discussed the project quite extensively. I shared the importance of autonomy of the national brothers. They have voted unanimously to go ahead and support the project without controls."

There's no guarantee you'll always have that kind of happy ending when you stand up for what's right. But it doesn't matter. God has called us to be here in the West, challenging the affluent people of this world to share with those in the most desperate need of all.

God is calling Christians in the West to recognize He is building His church as a caring, sharing and saving outreach to dying souls. He is using many North Americans who care about the lost to share in this new movement by supporting the native missionary leaders He has called to direct it.

God is calling the body of Christ in the affluent West to give up its proud, arrogant attitude of "our way is the only way" and share with those who will die in sin unless help is sent now from the richer nations. The West must share with the East, knowing that Jesus said, "Whatever you did for one of the least of these brothers of mine, you did for me" (Matt. 25:40, NIV).

Have native missionaries made mistakes? Yes. And it would be unwise stewardship to give away our money freely without knowledge of the truthfulness and integrity of any ministry. But that doesn't mean we shouldn't help the native missionary movement.

North America is at the crossroads. We can harden our hearts to the needs of the Third World — continuing in arrogance, pride and selfishness — or we can repent and move with the Spirit of God. Whichever way we turn, the laws of God will continue in effect.

If we close our hearts to the lost of the world who are dying and going to hell, we invite the judgment of God and a more certain ruin of our affluence. But if we open our hearts and share, it will be the beginning of new blessing and renewal.

This is why I believe that the response of North American believers to the cry of my heart is more than a missions question that can be shrugged off like another appeal letter or banquet invitation. Response to the needs of the lost world is directly tied to the spiritual beliefs and well-being of every believer.

Meanwhile, the unknown brethren of Asia continue to lift hands to God in prayer, asking Him to meet their needs. They are men and women of the highest caliber. They cannot be bought. Many have developed a devotion to God that makes them hate the idea of becoming servants of men and religious establishments for profit.

It is the highest privilege of affluent Christians in the West to share in their ministries by sending financial aid.

Without visible support, they are the true brethren of Christ about which the Bible speaks. Today they are walking from village to village facing beatings and persecution to bring Christ to Animists, Buddhists, communists, Hindus, Muslims and many other people who have still not received the good news of His love.

Without fear of men they are willing, like their Lord, to live as He did — sleeping on roadsides, going hungry and even dying in order to share their faith.

These are the men who go even though they may be told the mission fund is used up. They are determined to preach even though they know it will mean suffering. Why? Because they love the lost souls who are dying daily without Christ.

They are too busy doing the will of God to get involved in

186

church politics, board meetings, fund-raising campaigns and public relations efforts.

If we do not care enough to sponsor them — if we do not obey the love of Christ and send them support — we are sharing in the responsibility for those who go to eternal flames without ever hearing about the love of God. If native evangelists cannot go because no one will send them, the shame belongs to the body of Christ here because it has the funds to help them.

If those funds are not given to the Lord, they soon will disappear. If the Western church will not be a light to the world, the Lord will take the candlestick away.

Pretending the poor and lost don't exist may be an alternative. But averting our eyes from the truth will not eliminate our guilt.

Gospel for Asia exists to remind the affluent Christian that there is a hungry, needy, lost world of people out there whom Jesus loves and for whom He died. Will you join us in ministering to them?

21

A Third World Response

Those most concerned about missions have grown up hearing the classic approach of "send Americans" and never have been asked to consider alternatives better suited to changed geopolitical conditions. It is hard for some to hear me reinterpret the stories told by Western missionaries of hardship and fruitless ministry as indicators of outdated and inappropriate methods.

But the biggest hurdle for most North Americans is the idea that someone from somewhere else can do it better. Questions about our methods and safeguards for financial accountability, while often sincere and well-intentioned, sometimes emanate from a deep well of distrust and prejudice.

On one of my trips to the West Coast I was invited to meet with the mission committee of a church that supported over seventy-five American missionaries. After I shared our vision for supporting native missionaries, the committee chairman said, "We have been asked to support national missionaries before, but we haven't found a satisfactory way to hold these nationals accountable for either the money we send or the work they do." I sensed he spoke for the entire committee.

I could hardly wait to respond. This issue of accountability is the objection most often raised about supporting native missionaries to the Third World, and I can understand why. Indeed, I agree it is extremely important that there be adequate accountability in every area of ministry. Good stewardship demands it.

Then I detailed how we handle the subject.

"In order to make people accountable we need some norm by which to measure their performance," I said. "But what criteria should we use? Would the yearly independent audit our missionaries submit be adequate to see that they handled money wisely?"

In addition I raised other questions. "What about the churches they build or the projects they have undertaken? Should they be judged according to the patterns and goals some mission headquarters or denomination prescribed? What about the souls they've won and the disciples they've made? Would any denomination have criteria to evaluate those? How about criteria to evaluate their life-style on the field or the fruit they produce? Which of these categories should be used to make these native missionaries accountable?"

Those who had been leaning back in their chairs now were leaning forward.

I had laid a foundation for a thought I was sure they hadn't considered before. I continued: "Do you require the American missionaries you send overseas to be accountable to you? What criteria have you used in the past to account for the hundreds of thousands of dollars you have invested through the missionaries you support now?"

I looked to the chairman for an answer. He stumbled through a few phrases before admitting they never had thought of requiring American missionaries to be accountable nor was this ever a concern to them.

"The problem," I explained, "is not a matter of accountability but one of prejudice, mistrust and feelings of superiority. These are the issues that hinder love and support for our brothers in the Third World who are working to win their own people to Christ." I followed with this illustration.

"Three months ago I traveled to Asia to visit some of the brothers we support. In one country I met an American missionary who had for fourteen years been developing some social programs for his denomination. He had come to this country hoping he could establish his mission center. In this regard he had been successful. As I walked into his mission compound I passed a man with a gun, sitting at the gate. The compound was bordered by a number of buildings with at least half a dozen imported cars. The staff members were wearing Western clothes, and a servant was caring for one of the missionary children. The scene reminded me of a king living in a palace with his court of serfs caring for his every need. I had, in eighteen years of travel, seen this scene repeated many times," I explained.

"From conversation with some of the native missionaries, I learned that this American and his colleagues did live like kings with their servants and cars," I said. "They had no contact with the poor in the surrounding villages. While God's money is invested on missionaries like this who enjoy a life-style they could not afford in the United States — a life-style of a rich man, separated by economy and distance from the native missionaries walking barefoot, poorly dressed even by their own standards and sometimes going for days without eating. These nationals, in my opinion, are the real soldiers of the cross. Each one of the brothers we support in that country has established a church in less than twelve months, and some have started more than twenty churches in three years."

I told of another incident from my own country of India. Although India is closed to new missionaries, there are some Western missionaries living there from past times. And, of course, some denominations get a few new professional people in such as doctors or teachers. I was visiting one of the mission hospitals in India where some of these missionary doctors and their colleagues worked. All lived in richly furnished mansions. One had twelve servants to care for him and his family. One looked after the garden, another cared for the car, another cared for the children, two cooked in his kitchen, one took care of his family's clothes, and so on. And in eight years this missionary had won no one to Jesus nor established one church.

"What criteria," I dared to ask, "has been used by the two evangelical denominations that have sent these men to hold them accountable? In another place," I continued, "there is a hospital costing millions to build and more millions to keep staffed with Europeans and Americans where, in seventy-five years, not one living, New Testament church has been established. Did anyone ever ask for an account of such fruitless labor?

"These illustrations are not isolated instances," I assured them. "During my eighteen years of travel throughout Asia I have seen Western missionaries consistently living at an economic level many times above the people they work with. And the nationals working with them are treated like servants and live in poverty while these missionaries enjoy the luxuries of life."

I contrasted these examples with what the nationals are doing.

"Remember the illustration of the multi-million dollar hospital and no church?" I asked. "Well, four years ago we started supporting a native missionary and thirty co-workers who have started a mission only a few miles from the hospital. His staff has grown to 349 co-workers, and hundreds of churches have been started. Another native missionary, one of his co-workers, has established over thirty churches in three years. Where do these brothers live? In little huts just like the people with whom they work. I could give you hundreds of stories that illustrate the fruit of such dedicated lives. It is like the book of Acts being written once again.

"You are seeking accountability from native missionaries, accountability that is required for you to give them support? Remember that Jesus said, 'For John came neither eating nor drinking, and they say, He hath a devil. The Son of man came eating and drinking, and they say, Behold a man gluttonous, and a winebibber, a friend of publicans and sinners. But wisdom is justified of her children' [Matt. 11:18-19]."

Fruit, I pointed out, is the real test. " 'By their fruits ye shall know them,' Jesus said [Matt. 7:20].

"Paul told Timothy to do two things regarding his life. And these two things, I believe, are the biblical criteria for accountability. He told Timothy to watch his own life and to care for the ministry that was committed to him. The life of the missionary is the medium of his message."

Three hours had passed, yet the room remained quiet. I sensed I had their permission to continue.

"You asked me to give you a method to hold our native missionaries accountable. Apart from the issues I have raised, Gospel for Asia does have definite procedures to insure that we are good stewards of the monies and opportunities the Lord commits to us. But our requirements and methods reflect a different perspective and way of doing missions.

"First, Gospel for Asia assumes that we who are called are called to serve and not to be served. We walk before the millions of poor and destitute in Asia with our lives as an open testimony and example. I breathe, sleep and eat conscious of the perishing millions the Lord commands me to love and rescue."

Then I explained how God is reaching the lost, not through programs but through individuals whose lives are so committed to Him that He uses them as vessels to anoint a lost world. So we give top priority to how the missionaries and their leaders live. When we started to support one brother, he lived in two small rooms with concrete floors. He, his wife and four children slept on a mat on the floor. That was four years ago. On a recent visit to India I saw him living in the same place, sleeping on the same mat even though his staff had grown from 30 to 349 workers. He handles hundreds of thousands of dollars to keep this enormous ministry going, yet his life-style has not changed. The brothers he has drawn into the ministry are willing to die for Christ's sake because they have seen their leader sell out to Christ just as the apostle Paul did.

"In the West, people look to men with power and riches. In Asia our people look for men like Gandhi who, to inspire a following, was willing to give up all to become like the least of the poor. Accountability begins with the life of the missionary."

The second criteria we consider, I explained, is the fruitfulness of that life. Our investment of money shows in the result of lives changed and churches established. What greater accountability can we require?

When Western missionaries go into Third World countries, they are able to find nationals to follow them. But these nationals too often get caught up in denominational distinctives. Like produces like. Missionary leaders from denominations who fly into these countries and live in five-star hotels will draw to themselves so-called national leaders who are like themselves. Then, unfortunately, it is the so-called national leaders who are accused of wasting or misusing great amounts of money, while they have often merely followed the example provided by their Western counterparts.

Again I addressed the chairman: "Have you studied the lives and ministries of the American missionaries you support? I believe you will find that very few of them are directly involved in preaching Christ but are doing some sort of social work. If you apply the biblical principles I have outlined, I doubt you would support more than a handful of them."

Then I turned and asked the committee members to assess themselves. "If your life is not totally committed to Christ, you are not qualified to be on this committee. That means you cannot use your time, your talents or your money the way you want to. If you do and still think you can help direct God's people to reach a lost world, you mock God Himself. You have to evaluate how you spend every dollar and everything else you do in the light of eternity. The way each one of you lives is where we begin our crusade to reach the lost of this world."

I was gratified to see that the Lord spoke to many of them. There were tears and a feeling of Christ's awareness among us. This had been a painful time for me. I was glad when it was over.

22

Answers to Your Questions

One of the most educational and pleasurable moments for me in our meetings is the question-and-answer period. From the beginning of our ministry, I have found that a two-way exchange is an effective method to communicate with my audience.

Many ask about current conditions and Asian life-style. Others pose some very provocative questions which show they have been thinking seriously about the implications of the message. Some questions seek details about our policies and practices. Others deal with church growth or the strategy of the native missionary movement.

Certain questions come up repeatedly, and the following are my responses.

Question: What are the qualifications of missionaries you support?

Answer: By turning to the books of 1 and 2 Timothy in the New Testament, you will find a complete overview of the qualifications for a missionary evangelist.

However, there are five areas which I feel are especially important in the life of one applying to be a missionary evangelist:

Calling. We are not looking for hirelings, but for men of faith who are certain they are called to be an evangelist. *It's not a job.* A hireling quits when the going gets tough. We are not looking for a man who wants to represent a denomination, Gospel for Asia or K.P. Yohannan. We look for people who know they are called to represent Christ — people who will not seek to please men but God, seeking only God's glory, and who cannot be bought with money or influence. We are look- ing for people dedicated to winning whole nations to Christ — who believe in the Great Commission.

Walk. We are interested only in people who have a mature walk with the Lord. When the world sees such workers, they see the beauty of Jesus — the compassion and purity of our Lord. The only ones who can win others to Christ are men and women who are so lost in Jesus that they are like Him. This kind of person will not be a gossip or critical and judgmental of others. He is a person who is a giver, one who makes generosity and sharing a normal way of life. Most of all, this person has a love for the lost.

Life-style. Only people who live by kingdom principles can be successful native evangelists. This kind of person will live a life of righteousness and separation from the world. Such a person must be free from addiction to alcohol or drugs, free from lust and free from the love of money.

Fatherhood. Successful missionary evangelists are men whose wives and children love and respect them. If a man is not having a fruitful ministry in his own family, he can never plant churches. Such men will be modeling Christ to their own sons, and their ambition will be to send them someday to the most dangerous and neglected regions of their lands. They must model Christ to their families and dedicate their children to Christian service, raising them to minister. We cannot support a man who is not leading his family in the right way. Such a person is not qualified to preach.

Leadership. A successful native missionary is a man who loves the brethren and proves it with a servant spirit. He loves peace, is quick to forgive and is quick to ask forgiveness. Such a person knows how to cooperate and work with others, prays for them, and is a blessing to the group. This doesn't mean he is a compromiser. He loves the Word of God and correct doctrine and obeys the Scripture in all matters without question. A shepherd always is concerned about holding the flock together and protecting them, and this is what makes a missionary evangelist a productive church planter.

Question: What screening process do you use to select new native missionaries?

Answer: After we receive a completed application, inquiries are made among pastors and older Christian leaders who know the applicant and are able to evaluate him or her. Then, if the candidate is not already involved in ministry, he will be assigned an internship to work under an older missionary evangelist and become a "Timothy." As the disciple gains more experience and is able, he will do more and more outreach. When 1) support is pledged by a sponsor in the West, and 2) the intern is qualified and accepted by the mission board where he will be working, then he will go to the pioneer area where God is leading him to go.

Question: How are native missionary evangelists trained?

Answer: While we have several formal training programs, which I will explain in a moment, let me say that our most productive workers have not been trained in Bible schools or seminaries.

We have found in Asia that the best training is to use the disciple method Jesus used in New Testament days. This method is indigenous to our culture. Our most successful native missionaries are the ones who were trained on the field by older men whose life-style can be followed. These teachers are "born to reproduce."

Disciples are made on the field, not in the classroom. It is dangerous to isolate the leadership and train them in sterile and artificial situations away from the masses of people in our villages. (This is why I especially oppose bringing most native missionaries to the West for training.)

Therefore, we have been funding and supporting missionary training programs which are short-term and involve internship with actual local churches. A missionary trainee will have the opportunity to attend classroom sessions as well as implement his studies in local evangelism. The mobile evangelistic team is still one of the best methods to combine training and outreach at the same time. Before a church planting assignment is given a missionary, I believe he needs to have some time doing intensive evangelism.

All this is supplemented by annual and regional conferences held throughout the area where native missionaries gather for prayer, Bible teaching and fellowship.

Question: To whom are native missionary evangelists accountable?

Answer: In almost all cases, they are being supervised by local indigenous mission boards or elders under whom they work. It is the quality of field leadership which is at the core of all accountability in Gospel for Asia.

On my frequent journeys to Asia, I spend much of my time meeting with the leaders of these indigenous missions in the various nations where we are working. Sometimes I will play a role in forming new boards — usually on a state or regional basis. But we want no operating control over the day-to-day affairs of these autonomous missions.

In searching for local mission boards on the field, my staff and I look for certain characteristics:

First, I look for boards that are made up of older, godly leaders who have successfully planted churches themselves and are proven evangelists.

Second, I look for men who are willing to meet regularly with the native missionaries for prayer, fellowship and sharing.

Third, I look for men who are not sectarian in outlook. We are not eager to spread any one particular denominational or doctrinal position.

Fourth, I look for men who live a life of simplicity, purity, holiness, love and faithfulness to the work.

Finally, I avoid boards that are controlled by men with a power-hungry attitude.

However, I do expect men on the board to be looking out for two things in the lives of the native evangelists we support: life-style and doctrine according to 2 Timothy 4:16. I believe that by simply reading 1 and 2 Timothy you get a pretty good idea of how a person is qualified to be a missionary evangelist.

In this sense, the local boards are responsible to see that native missionaries are qualified when they are first approved for support and remain so throughout their years of service.

Question: What about grand strategy? Who is directing the efforts of the native missionaries?

Answer: Experienced elders help make these kinds of tactical decisions. But in the day-to-day affairs of the work we are trusting the Holy Spirit to guide us about where to go and when. The native missionaries must wait on God for personal direction. If they cannot do this, they are not ready to be released into the field.

Question: What are the methods used by native mission-aries?

Answer: While films, radio, television and video are becoming more common in Asia, the most effective methods still sound more as if they came from the book of Acts!

The most effective evangelism is done face-to-face in the streets. Most native missionaries walk or ride bicycles between villages much as the Methodist circuit riders did in America's frontier days. A bicycle is one of the most important tools any native evangelist can own.

Street preaching and open-air evangelism, often using World

War II style megaphones, is the most common way to proclaim the gospel. Sometimes evangelists arrange witnessing parades and/or tent campaigns and distribute simple gospel tracts during week-long village crusades.

Since the majority of the world's one billion illiterates live in Asia, the gospel often must be proclaimed to them without using literature. This is done with small hand-cranked card-talk phonographs, cassette tapes, flip charts and films.

Kowvali songfests, a folk tradition, are popular in the villages of North India. Lasting for hours, they attract large crowds. In a Kowvali, the leader tells a story in song while pumping the bellows of a harmonium. A chorus of friends, chanting humorous responses, plays drums and rattles. A number of gospel and Bible stories have been adapted to this medium, and it is a good example of effective evangelism coming out of northwest India.

Trucks, vans, primitive loud-speaker systems, bicycles, leaflets, pamphlets, books, banners and flags are the most important tools. Easy to use and train with, they now are being supplemented with radio broadcasting, cassette players, film projectors and television.

These types of communication tools are available in Asia at low cost, and the native evangelists are familiar with them. They don't shock the culture, and we can buy them locally without paying import duties.

Question: Are native missionaries prepared to carry on cross-cultural evangelism?

Answer: Yes, with great effectiveness. Most of the native missionaries we support, for example, are involved in cross-cultural evangelism. Often, GFA evangelists find they must learn a new language, plus adopt different dress and dietary customs. However, since the cultures are frequently neighbors or share a similar heritage, the transition is much easier than it would be for someone coming from the West.

Even though my homeland has sixteen major languages and

1,650 dialects — each representing a different culture — it is still relatively easy for an Indian to make a transition from one culture to the other. In fact, almost anyone in Pakistan, India, Bangladesh, Burma, Nepal, Bhutan, Thailand and Sri Lanka can rather quickly cross-minister into a neighboring culture.

Question: What kind of churches are native evangelists planting?

Answer: First of all, and most important, indigenous missionaries establish local congregations which are part of the life-style and needs of the country and community they serve. We're not using Western labels and building churches along denominational traditions. Why should we be concerned about denominational names when most of the people haven't yet heard the name of Jesus?

We believe that Christ came to change the hearts of our people, not our culture. So we are concentrating our energies on building congregations which spring out of our own way of life.

Most evangelists in the native missionary movement will call their new congregations after the name of the village or perhaps some place in the Bible.

The building may be of stone or mud, or it may be just a roof of coconut or banana leaves. There are no benches or chairs. Straw mats are spread over the ground so the congregation may sit. The people usually are divided into three groups — the children sit in front, the men on one side and the women on the other.

As you approach a service in progress, the singing and handclapping can be heard from a distance. Usually it is accompanied by drums, tambourines, rattles and other local instruments.

The words of the songs, sung in native dialects, reflect a specific situation in the life of the believer — giving them immediate meaning to all who participate and hear.

Each believer has a part in the service, which usually begins with one or two hours of worship and singing. One after another, believers stand to testify about what the Lord has done for them during the past week. There is much joy in this kind of meeting, and it is likely to last three or four hours.

Frequently, there may be two sermons presented. The approach to the Scriptures is made in reverence. The goal is not to study them in order to isolate doctrines, but to learn how God would have the new believer walk.

This kind of native church service is very different from worship in the West, yet it serves the same purpose — to allow believers to worship God, to be a witness to the community, to live the Christian life better and to bring many souls to Christ. It is the liturgy of a growing church determined to reach out to the lost masses.

Question: In light of the fact that you will be needing at least 200,000 missionaries to reach Asia, are there enough missionaries available to do the work?

Answer: The answer is yes. Since the current movement began, we never have had a problem finding enough native missionary evangelists. Right now we know of ten thousand evangelists on the field who need support to improve their ministry — with bicycles, bull horns, Christian literature, and so on. By the time these ten thousand are sponsored, I believe we will have another ten thousand waiting.

An amazing phenomenon is taking place throughout what I call the real Asia. At the village level, where masses of people live and die in anonymous poverty, God is doing a supernatural work. Hundreds of thousands are coming to Christ. And as fast as they do, they are being formed into little worshipping cells of believers. There the native missionary evangelists are able to train new disciples to take their place so they can multiply the work in new villages. As we have the support, these new disciples can go into the harvest fields themselves as evangelists.

Many of these new converts are willing to give up their jobs in order to take the gospel to the unreached. Plainly, there is no shortage of people power in Asia. The need is for money to send these workers out properly trained and equipped.

Question: With your emphasis on the native missionary movement, don't you feel there is still a place for Western missionaries in Asia?

Answer: Yes, there still are places for Western missionaries. First, there are still countries with no existing church from which to draw native missionaries. Morocco, Afghanistan and the Maldives Islands come to mind. In these places, missionaries from outside — whether from the West, Africa or Asia — are the only possible way the gospel can be spread.

Second, Christians in the West have technical skills which may be needed by their brothers and sisters in Third World churches. The work of Wycliffe Bible Translators is a good example. Their help in translation efforts in the nearly forty-five hundred languages still without a Bible is invaluable. So when Third World churches invite Westerners to come and help them, and the Lord is in it, the Westerner obviously should respond.

Third, there are short-term discipleship experiences that I think are especially valuable. Organizations like Operation Mobilization and Youth With a Mission have had a catalytic impact on both Asian and Western churches. These are discipleship-building ministries that benefit the Western participants as well as Asia's unevangelized millions.

Also, it must be noted that OM, headed by George Verwer, has recruited thousands of young people from India and other Asian nations for discipleship training with an emphasis on literature evangelism.

During the last twenty years, OM has done more to challenge the church in India (and other Asian nations) for pioneer evangelism among the most unreached than any other group I know. I personally was recruited by the brothers of OM in 1966 to go to North India.

Through cross-cultural and interracial contact, such ministries are especially helpful because they allow Westerners to get a better understanding of the situation in Asia. Alumni of these programs are helping others in the West understand the real needs of the Third World.

And, of course, there is the simple fact that the Holy Spirit does call individuals from one culture to witness in another. When He calls, we should respond.

Question: Why don't indigenous churches support their own missionaries in the Third World?

Answer: They do. In fact, I believe most Asian Christians give a far greater portion of their income to missions than do Americans. Scores of times, I have seen them give chicken eggs, rice, mangos and tapioca roots, since they frequently don't have cash. The fact of the matter is, growing churches of Asia are made up of people from the poor masses. Often they simply don't have money. These are people from among that one-fourth of the world's population who live on just a few dollars each week.

Many times we find that a successful missionary evangelist will be almost crippled by his own dynamic growth. When a great move of the Holy Spirit occurs in a village, the successful missionary may find he has trained several gifted co-workers as "Timothys" who are ready to establish sister congregations. However, the rapid growth almost always outstrips the original congregation's ability to support additional staff. This is where outside help is vitally needed.

As God's Spirit continues to move, many new mission boards are being formed. Some of the largest missionary societies in the world are now located in Asia. For example, at the time of the revision of this book in 1992, Gospel for Asia alone was helping to support seven thousand native missionary staff members — and this number is increasing at an astonishing rate. But in light of the need, we literally need hundreds of thousands of additional missionaries who will in turn require more outside support.

Regrettably, there are some indigenous churches which don't support native evangelists for the same reason some American congregations don't give — lack of vision and sin in the lives of the pastors and congregations. But this is no excuse for American Christians to sit back and lose the greatest opportunity they've ever had to help win a lost world to Jesus.

Question: Is there a danger that native missionary sponsorships will have a reverse effect by causing native evangelists to depend on the West for support rather than turning to the local churches?

Answer: The truth is, of course, that it is not outside money that weakens a growing church, but outside *control*. Money from the West actually liberates the evangelists right now and makes it possible for them to follow the call of God.

After generations of domination by Western colonialists, most Asians are acutely conscious of the potential problem of foreign control through outside money. It is frequently brought up in discussions by native missionary leaders, and most native missionary boards have developed policies and practices to provide for accountability without foreign control.

In Gospel for Asia, we have taken several steps to make sure money gets to the local missionary evangelist in a responsible way without destroying valuable local autonomy.

First, our selection and training process is designed to favor men and women who begin with a right attitude — missionaries who are dependent on God for their support rather than on men. In fact, many of the native missionaries we support have worked for long periods in near-starvation situations before any support has arrived.

Second, there is no direct or indirect supervision of the work by Western supporters. The donor gives the Lord's money to the missionary through Gospel for Asia, and we in turn send the money to his board. GFA does not usually send the money directly to a native missionary but to a group of leaders who oversee the financial affairs on each field. Therefore, the native evangelist is twice-removed from the source of funds. This procedure is being followed by several other organizations which are collecting funds in the West for native support, and it seems to work very well.

Finally, as soon as a new work is established, the native missionary should be moving on to begin in another area. The new congregation usually has enough financial responsibility to support the gospel worker he leaves behind, but they still are giving sacrificially to support evangelism. Eventually, I am sure the native churches will be able to support most pioneer evangelism, but the job is too big now without Western aid.

The quickest way to help Asian churches become self-supporting, I believe, is to support a growing native missionary movement. As new churches are planted, the blessings of the gospel will abound, and the new Asian believers will be able to support greater outreach. Sponsorship monies are like investment capital in the work of God. The best thing we can do to help make the Asian church independent now is to support as many native missionaries as possible.

Question: How can Gospel for Asia support a native missionary evangelist for only $360 to $1,200 a year when my church says it takes $43,000 to support an American missionary on the same fields?

Answer: There is a vast difference between living at the same level as an Asian peasant — as native evangelists do — and living at even a modest Western standard. In most of the nations where we support local missionaries, they are able to survive on one to three dollars a day. This is approximately the same per capita income of the people to whom they are ministering in most cases.

A North American missionary, however, is faced with many

additional costs. These include international air transportation, language schools, special English-language schools for children, and Western-style housing. Native missionaries, on the other hand, live in villages on the same level as others in the community whom they are seeking to reach for Christ.

The Western missionary also is faced with visa and other legal fees, costs of communication with donors, extra medical care, import duties, and requirements to pay Social Security and income taxes back in the States. The cost of food can be very high, especially if the missionary entertains other Westerners, employs servants to cook, and eats imported foods. Frequently, host governments require foreign missionaries to meet special tax or reporting requirements, usually with payments required.

Clothing, such as shoes and imported Western garments, is costly. Many native missionaries choose to wear sandals and dress as the local people do.

For a Western missionary family with children, the pressure is intense to maintain a semblance of American-style living. Frequently this is increased by peer pressure at private schools where other students are the sons and daughters of international businessmen and diplomats.

Finally, vacations and in-country travel or tourism are not considered essential by native missionaries as they are by most Americans. The cost of imported English books, periodicals, records and tapes is also a big expense not part of a native missionary's life-style.

The result of all this is that American missionaries often need thirty to forty times more money for their support than does a native missionary.

Question: It seems as if I'm getting fund-raising appeals every day from good Christian organizations. How can I know who is genuine and really in the center of God's will?

Answer: Many Christians receive appeal letters each month from all kinds of religious organizations.

Obviously, you can't respond to all the appeals, so what criteria should you use to make your decision? Here are a few guidelines we have developed for missions giving which I believe will help:

• Do those asking for money believe in the fundamental truths of God's Word, or are they liberal theologically? Any mission that seeks to carry out God's work must be totally committed to His Word. Is the group asking for money affiliated with liberal organizations which deny the truth of the gospel, while keeping the name "Christian"? Do their members openly declare their beliefs? Too many today walk in a gray area, taking no stands, trying to offend as few as possible so they can get money from all, whether friends or enemies of the cross of Christ. The Word of God is being fulfilled in them: "...having a form of godliness, but denying the power thereof" (2 Tim. 3:5).

• Is the goal of their mission to win souls, or are they only social-gospel oriented? One of the biggest lies the devil uses to send people to hell is, How can we preach the gospel to a man with an empty stomach? Because of this lie, for a hundred years much of missions money has been invested in social work rather than in spreading the Word.

Ask before you give, Is this mission involved in preaching the gospel of Jesus Christ? The liberal believes man is basically good; therefore, all that is needed to solve his problems is to change his environment. The Bible says all — rich and poor — must repent and come to Christ or be lost. Which gospel is being preached by the mission group asking for your support? (I have explained this in greater detail elsewhere in this book.)

• Is the mission organization financially accountable? Do they use the money for the purpose for which it was given? At Gospel for Asia every penny given for support of a missionary is sent to the field for that purpose. Our home office is supported with funds given for that purpose. Are their finances audited by independent auditors according to accepted procedures? Will they send an audited financial statement to anyone requesting it? Gospel for Asia meets both standards.

• Do members of the mission group live by faith or by man's wisdom? God never changes His plan: "The just shall live by faith." When a mission continually sends out crisis appeals for its maintenance rather than for outreach, there is something wrong with it. They seem to say God made a commitment, but now He is in trouble, and we must help Him out of some tight spot. God makes no promises He cannot keep. If a mission group constantly begs and pleads for money, you need to ask if they are doing what God wants them to do. We believe we must wait upon God for His mind and do only what He leads us to do, instead of taking foolish steps of faith without His going before us. The end should never justify the means.

• Finally, a word of caution. Don't look for a reason for not giving to the work of God. Remember, we must give all we can, keeping only enough to meet our needs so the gospel can be preached "before the night comes and no man can work." The problem for most is not that we give too much, but that we give too little. We live selfishly and store up treasures on this earth which will be destroyed soon, while precious souls die and go to hell.

Question: How can I sponsor a native missionary evangelist?

Answer: There are several American-based organizations, including Gospel for Asia, that now are channeling support to the native missionary movement. It is not advisable to send money directly to the field, since agencies like ours have elaborate systems to evaluate, train and hold local missionaries accountable.

To sponsor a native missionary through Gospel for Asia, here's all you need do:

• Write Gospel for Asia using the tear-out coupon at the end of this book. Let us know you want to help sponsor a native missionary.

• Enclose your first pledge payment. Most of our friends sponsor missionaries for between $30 and $120 a month.

• As soon as you receive information about your missionary, pray for him and his family every day.

Question: Are financial records audited on the field?

Answer: Yes, we inspect financial records to ensure that funds are used according to the purpose intended. A detailed accounting in writing is required for projects such as village crusades, training conferences and special programs. Missionary support funds are signed for as received both by leaders and the missionaries involved, and these receipts are checked.

All financial records on the field are also audited annually by certified public accountants.

Epilogue

Even as our ministry has expanded and grown, my own life has not become easier. I am now traveling halfway around the world half a dozen times a year meeting with our leaders on the field. In addition, when I am in the United States, I am often on speaking tours of up to two weeks' duration. In fact, in one recent year I spoke in ninety cities across the country.

Without the spiritual support of my wife, Gisela, it would not be humanly possible for me to keep up the pace. But she encourages me so completely that I keep on going. In fact, there are times when I am so weary I feel I cannot face another trip, and I feel bad for leaving my family again. But Gisela urges me to go because it is what the Lord has called me to do, and she sustains me with her prayers.

Our life as a couple, and as a family, is consumed with one thought: to do everything we can to support the native missionaries as they seek to win the lost millions of Asia to Christ. Eternity is very real to us. We evaluate everything we do against the reality of the millions who will perish forever unless we reach them with the gospel.

So we have made a deliberate decision to suffer so the gospel can be furthered. This decision was not enjoined upon us — we make it daily with prayerful joy. We have continued to maintain a simple life-style. We have made a covenant not to save up riches or accumulate the things of this world for our children, but that everything we have should be continually spent to reach the lost souls who have never heard the name of Jesus.

And in this life we must go on, until we see the Lord face to face.

A while ago, as I put my children to bed, as usual each one took his or her turn to pray. But that night my son, Daniel, age nine, added a new sentence to his prayers: "...and, Jesus, please help me to be a missionary."

A few days later, Sarah, age six, also prayed the same prayer. From the day they were born we prayed that the Lord would save them and call them to be missionaries and follow in their parents' footsteps.

In everything we do in our family, we teach our children to ask: What will this do to help us further the gospel by helping our brothers on the field who are going through much suffering in their commitment to preach?

We acknowledge we are in a real spiritual war, with millions of lives at stake to spend eternity without God.

Sometimes I think I am a madman, but then I know it is not madness as some may think — it is a total obedience to Christ and His call. I believe this is a normal life-style for anyone who seeks to follow Him, knowing that time will soon run out, and eternity is real.

A Prayer

Dear Lord, we acknowledge that our commitment to You is so shallow. We say we love You, but our actions betray us.

Open our eyes so that we see time and eternity as You see them. Forgive us for forgetting we are only strangers and pilgrims on this earth.

How foolish we are, O Lord, to store up treasures on this earth and fight to save our lives and preserve them, when You tell us we will lose our lives if we try to do that.

We ask You, dear Lord, to forgive us and help us to walk in Your footsteps — forsaking all, denying ourselves, carrying our crosses daily and loving You supremely so Your causes might be furthered in this dark and dying world.

In Jesus' name, Amen.

Notes

Chapter 4

1. Robert L. Heilbroner, *The Great Ascent: The Struggle for Economic Development in Our Time* (New York: Harper & Row, 1963), pp. 33-36.

Chapter 5

1. Rochunga Pudaite, *My Billion Bible Dream* (Nashville: Thomas Nelson Publishers, 1982), p. 129.
2. Ref. (Pasadena: U.S. Center for World Mission)

Chapter 8

1. 1980 World Population Data Sheet, Population Reference Bureau, 1337 Connecticut Avenue, N.W., Washington, D.C.

Chapter 10

1. William McDonald, *True Discipleship* (Kansas City: Walterick Publishers, 1975), p. 31.

Chapter 11

1. C. Peter Wagner, *On the Crest of the Wave* (Ventura: Regal Books, 1983), p. 150.
2. Watchman Nee, *Love Not the World* (Fort Washington: Christian Literature Crusade, 1968), pp. 23, 24.

Chapter 12

1. A.W. Tozer, *Of God and Man* (Harrisburg: Christian Publications Inc., 1960), p. 35.

Chapter 14

1. *India Journal*, published by Bibles for India, 1984.
2. David B. Barrett, *World Christian Encyclopedia* (New York: Oxford University Press, 1982), pp. 133, 135.
3. *Ibid.*, pp. 165, 166.
4. *Ibid.*, pp. 179, 180.
5. *Ibid.*, pp. 202-204.
6. *Ibid.*, pp. 360-363.
7. *Ibid.*, pp. 381-388.
8. *Ibid.*, pp. 419-426.
9. *Ibid.*, pp. 440-445.
10. *Ibid.*, pp. 472-476.
11. *Ibid.*, pp. 476-477.
12. *Ibid.*, pp. 507-508.
13. *Ibid.*, pp. 542-545.
14. *Ibid.*, pp. 562-568.
15. *Ibid.*, pp. 613-616.
16. *Ibid.*, pp. 634-638.
17. *Ibid.*, pp. 235-238.
18. *Ibid.*, pp. 664-667.

Chapter 16

1. Allen Finley, Lorry Lutz, *Mission: A World-Family Affair* (San Jose: Christian National Press, 1981), pp. 38, 39.

Chapter 17

1. Dennis E. Clark, *The Third World and Mission* (Waco: Word Books, 1971), p. 70.
2. C. Peter Wagner, *On the Crest of the Wave* (Ventura: Regal Books, 1983), p. 93.
3. Roland Allen, *The Spontaneous Expansion of the Church* (Grand Rapids: William B. Eerdmans, 1962), p. 19.

Chapter 18

1. George Verwer, *No Turning Back* (Wheaton: Tyndale House Publishers, 1983), pp. 89, 90.

Why Not Share This Exciting Book With Others?

...your family...your church...your pastor
...your friends...your Bible study group

Now available in pocket-size edition for only $1!

Call toll free today to order your copies:
1-800-WIN-ASIA
(1-800-946-2742)
(in the USA or Canada)

Or mail the coupon below with your payment to:
Gospel for Asia
USA: 1932 Walnut Plaza, Carrollton, TX 75006
Canada: P.O. Box 4000, Waterdown, ONT L0R 2H0

✂ — — — — — — — — — — — — — — — — — — —

Yes, please send me _____ copies of *Revolution in World Missions* at $1 each.

Total enclosed $_____

Name_____

Address_____

City_____

State/Province_____

ZIP/Postal Code_____

Telephone (_____)_____

H925-PB10

S921-WCB1

You Can Become a Sender!

Yes! I care about the lost and forgotten millions of Asia. I will help native missionaries reach their own people for Jesus. I understand that it takes $30 to $120 per month to support a native missionary fully, depending on his or her marital status, family size and location of service.

To begin sponsoring today call toll free:
1-800-WIN-ASIA
(1-800-946-2742)
(in the USA or Canada)

Or mail the coupon on the back of this page to:

Gospel for Asia
USA: 1932 Walnut Plaza, Carrollton, TX 75006
Canada: P.O. Box 4000, Waterdown, ONT L0R 2H0
Germany: Karsauer Str. 15A, D7888 Rheinfelden

*You will receive a photo and testimony of each
native missionary you help sponsor.*

**Gospel for Asia sends 100% of your
missionary support to the mission field.**
Nothing is taken out for administrative expenses.

All donations are tax-deductible.

H925-RB1S

S921-WCB1

You Can Become a Sender!

☐ Starting now I will prayerfully help sponsor:

    ☐ 1 missionary at:

        ☐ $120 monthly

        ☐ $90 monthly

        ☐ $60 monthly

        ☐ $30 monthly

        ☐ $_____ monthly

    ☐ _____ missionaries at $_____ each monthly

       (total $_____ monthly)

    Total enclosed $_____

☐ **Please send me more information** about how to help
   sponsor a native missionary, including a FREE
   one-year subscription to *SEND!* — the newspaper
   voice of native missions.

Name_____

Address_____

City_____

State/Province_____

ZIP/Postal Code_____

Telephone (_____)_____

HELP US INVOLVE OTHERS

Give your Christian friends and relatives a FREE subscription to *SEND!* — the voice of native missions. Help give them a missions vision! Just fill out their names and addresses below. Use additional sheets of paper if necessary. Please print clearly.

❖❖❖❖❖❖❖❖❖❖❖❖❖❖❖❖❖❖❖❖❖❖❖

Name_____

Address_____ Apt. #_____

City_____ State_____

ZIP Code_____ Telephone (_____)_____

❖❖❖❖❖❖❖❖❖❖❖❖❖❖❖❖❖❖❖❖❖❖❖

Name_____

Address_____ Apt. #_____

City_____ State_____

ZIP Code_____ Telephone (_____)_____

❖❖❖❖❖❖❖❖❖❖❖❖❖❖❖❖❖❖❖❖❖❖❖

☐ Please identify me as the gift subscription donor. My name is

_____

Please send your list of mission-minded friends to:
Gospel for Asia
USA: 1932 Walnut Plaza, Carrollton, TX 75006
Canada: P.O. Box 4000, Waterdown, ONT L0R 2H0

F925-PB10

S921-WCB1